1989

P-23 - Settlement locations
   4. Ghost towns

23149 JA - Canada. 1941

TWO MONOGRAPHS
ON JAPANESE CANADIANS

*This is a volume in the
Arno Press collection*

THE ASIAN EXPERIENCE
IN NORTH AMERICA

Chinese and Japanese

Advisory Editor
Roger Daniels

Editorial Board
Gordon Hirabayashi
Harry H.L. Kitano
H. Brett Melendy
Howard Palmer
Betty Lee Sung

*See last pages of this volume
for a complete list of titles*

TWO MONOGRAPHS ON JAPANESE CANADIANS

Edited by Roger Daniels

ARNO PRESS
A New York Times Company
New York • 1978

Publisher's Note: This book has been reproduced from the best available copies.

Reprint Edition 1978 by Arno Press Inc.

Arrangement and compilation copyright 1978 by Arno Press Inc.

"A History of the Japanese Canadians in British Columbia 1877 to 1958" by Ken Adachi was reprinted by permission of The National Japanese Canadian Citizens Association.
"Canadian Japanese in Southern Alberta: 1905-1945" by David Iwaasa was reprinted by permission of the author.

THE ASIAN EXPERIENCE IN NORTH AMERICA: Chinese and Japanese
ISBN for complete set: 0-405-11261-0
See last pages of this volume for titles.

Manufactured in the United States of America

Library of Congress Cataloging in Publication Data

Main entry under title:

Two monographs on Japanese Canadians.

(The Asian experience in North America : Chinese and Japanese)
Reprint of the 1958 ed. of K. Adachi's A history of the Japanese Canadians in British Columbia, 1877-1958, and of the 1972 ed. of D. Iwaasa's Canadian Japanese in southern Alberta, 1905-1945, which was published by the University of Lethbridge, Lethbridge, Alta., in series: University of Lethbridge research paper.
  1. Japanese in British Columbia--History.
2. Japanese in Alberta--History. 3. British Columbia--History. 4. Alberta--History.
I. Daniels, Roger. II. Adachi, Ken. A history of the Japanese Canadians in British Columbia, 1877-1958. 1978. III. Iwaasa, David B. Canadian Japanese in southern Alberta, 1905-1945. 1978. IV. Series. V. Series: University of Lethbridge. University of Lethbridge research paper.
F1089.7.J3T96   971.1'004'956   78-3222
ISBN 0-405-11304-8

CONTENTS

Adachi, Ken
A HISTORY OF THE JAPANESE CANADIANS IN BRITISH COLUMBIA, 1877-1958, [Toronto], 1958

Iwaasa, David
CANADIAN JAPANESE IN SOUTHERN ALBERTA: 1905-1945, Lethbridge, Canada, 1972

A

HISTORY

OF THE JAPANESE CANADIANS

IN BRITISH COLUMBIA

1877 - 1958

** **** **

KEN ADACHI

** **** **

WRITTEN UNDER THE AUSPICES OF THE HISTORY COMMITTEE OF
THE NATIONAL JAPANESE CANADIAN CITIZENS ASSOCIATION

1958

This short history is one of the first steps towards accomplishing the writing of a book-length national History of the Japanese Canadians. As such, it is only a factual account of Japanese Canadians in British Columbia and does not attempt to relate or analyse all of the many events that have occurred. The National JCCA hopes to publish a comprehensive History combined with first person accounts of some of of the episodes in the near future.

TABLE OF CONTENTS

PREFACE iv

I.   THE BEGINNINGS
     1. The Arrival 1
     2. Economic Expansion 6
     3. The Rising Tide of Discrimination 9
     4. The Society 12

II   PEARL HARBOUR AND EVACUATION
     1. The Established Notions 16
     2. Pressure and Policy 19
     3. The Removal 21
     4. The Ghost Towns 23
     5. Nisei Enlistment 25

III. AFTER THE EVACUATION: THE ISSUES
     1. Dispersal and Relocation 27
     2. The Repatriation Issue 28
     3. The Property Problem 32

IV. RETURN AND RE-ESTABLISHMENT 35

CONCLUSION 41

BIBLIOGRAPHY 44

Copyright 1958 by
National Japanese Canadian Citizens Association

All rights reserved. No part of this History may be reproduced in any form without the written permission of the National Japanese Canadian Citizens Association History Committee.

PREFACE

Home to those immigrants who settled down, and the children who were born to them, was this evergreen province with its infinite variety. Home was the silent lakes, the brown, rushing rivers, the small manicured strawberry plots, the smoky woods, the rock-strewn defiles of the mountains, the rain and fog of the cities nestled along the Pacific. Their hopes and dreams were bound up in British Columbia.

But the promise of a brave new world was not theirs to be fulfilled. True, there were goodly people, but the white foam of discrimination and mistrust bubbled about them. And to sink their roots, to quell the scalding cry of the spirit, the agony of their souls, was not easy.

Then there was the evacuation, surely one of the most turbulent periods in the history of the province. And it was sad and bitter to be pushed out like troublesome boarders as if they were not part of the country. Whether the results achieved justified the tremendous expenditure of governmental effort, the taxpayer's money, and the large cost in mental anguish and economic loss of so many people, can best be judged for oneself. This wholesale unrooting and its aftermath is not one of the brighter chapters in the province's history; but it is one that cannot be erased or whitewashed.

The story of the Japanese in British Columbia, of all the groups in the province, is easily the most dramatic, and disturbing in its ramifications. It would take a rather fat volume to tell all the stormy story, a story that is unparalleled in Canadian history. No attempt is made here to cover all the details; in this brief length, this is but a study of broad movements and developments. No attempt, too, is made to raise moral judgments; the facts, as given here, should stand up.

The story of British Columbia's Japanese Canadians is unique. Withal, they have had their loves and lusts, their strengths and weaknesses, their long days of lonliness and fear. Many have gone eastward after the storm, never to return; others have come back. But for all, the roaring sound of rivers, the rustle of autumn leaves underfoot, the strange music of an embattled street, the giant timber reaching skyward presaging a promise, remain in the mind's eye. The memories of the long years are both good and bad.

I THE BEGINNINGS

1. The Arrival

The story of the Japanese in B.C. begins with the arrival of a small number of immigrants, following upon the emergence of Japan into the modern world from its feudal cocoon in 1867. Around 1884, small numbers of Japanese began to arrive in B.C., though for a decade, only about 1,000 Japanese were in Canada. It was from 1896 onwards that immigration began on a significant scale, and they came in ever-increasing waves until by the turn of the century 4,738 Japanese were in Canada, 97 percent in B.C.

What attracted the Japanese to B.C.? Like any other immigrant group, the Japanese were drawn by the prospect of plentiful work and quick returns. The province was going through a period of economic expansion and development in which they could find easy access to employment. This prompted the immigrants to seek a quick fortune in B.C., and after this hope was grounded, to make a permanent home there. Again, the proximity of Japan to B.C. and its agreeable mild green climate made them settle in Canada's westernmost province. Only a negligible number resided outside of B.C. from the early days up to 1941.

It is generally accepted that the first Japanese to reach Canada was a highly enterprising and energetic sailor, Manzo Nagano. Nineteen when he arrived at New Westminster in 1877, Nagano was to spend the greatest part of 46 years in B.C. until finally he returned to Nagasaki in 1923. On his first trip to B.C., Nagano remained ashore, and with an Italian partner, spent two years in fishing on the Fraser River, the first of many Japanese to make a livelihood in this industry. In 1880 Nagano went on to Vancouver--or Gastown as it was more commonly known--where he worked as a lumberman.

He returned to the Orient, coming back in 1884 on a ship which was transporting 500 Chinese labourers from Hong Kong to Port Moody. Nagano continued his itinerant life, touching again at New Westminster where he found about seven or eight Japanese engaged in fishing, and passing through Steveston where there were five Japanese living. He went to Seattle, and established a cigarette stand and restaurant; but again returned to Japan after a few years. In 1892 he was in Victoria where he opened a store dealing in Japanese novelties and goods. A few years later, he occupied himself in salting salmon and exporting it to Japan, especially to Hokkaido where the demand was great, realizing a tidy profit. Eventually, he brought a wife from Japan to Victoria, expanded his novelty store, opened a hotel, and organized a Japanese social club. During World War I when the Japanese warship "Izumo" docked at Esquimalt, Nagano presented some Canadian trees to the captain to be planted in Japan.

Thus Nagano's activities in B.C. indicate the peculiar kind of enterprise and industriousness for which the Japanese soon became noted, and for which they came to be feared. The later settlers, however, were neither nomadic or as successful as Nagano. For most of them, hopes of a quick fortune were soon dissipated, and they had to adjust themselves to the new life, gradually to sink roots deeper into the new soil. They were a hardy lot, these early pioneers, hard and strong and vital.

Another early arrival, Yasukichi Yoshizawa, became closely associated with the native Indians of the northern coast of B.C., and spoke their language freely. He is credited with opening up fishing for the Japanese in northern waters because he was the first to go as far north as the Skeena to investigate fishing conditions there. He set out in April 8, 1891, in a small boat, after quitting his job with the Hastings Lumber Mill in Vancouver, to take a look at the Northern coast. It took Yoshizawa and four others 42 days to reach the mouth of the Skeena, and they were met with amazement by the local inhabitants who had never seen a Japanese before. They found jobs in a cannery, and encouraged other Japanese to the district. Almost all of those early pioneers are dead; but what stories they would have had to tell.

During the turn of the century, new rail lines surged through the Rockies, and the rich resources of the coastal areas-- the salmon, the minerals, the timber, and the land--were being tapped. The demand for manual labour in B.C. could not be met by immigrants from the remote Atlantic seaboard; the countries across the Pacific alone could provide sufficient manpower. Large Canadian concerns induced the immigrants to come under contract from the Orient. Two of these were the Wellington Colliery Company and the Canadian Pacific Railway. And so it was that there was the curious sight of Japanese immigrants working on the CPR, some of them wearing frock coats and top hats, shovel in hand. Such incongruity could only make them conspicuous, and consequently, one immigrant wryly relates "they couldn't be lazy".

At any rate, the contribution of these immigrants toward the early economic development of B.C. was noteworthy. A large number of them, however, remained in Canada only a short time: some moved on to the U.S. before 1901, some had come only as seasonal workers, many returned to Japan in disenchantment because of the rising tide of hostility and prejudice directed against them. As early as 1891, an attempt was made to introduce an anti-Japanese measure in the Legislature of B.C. by an amendment to a motion to increase the Chinese Head Tax from fifty to two hundred dollars and extending it to include the Japanese. This was only the first in a series of legislative attempts to enact laws of a restrictive nature, reflecting the sentiment of public unrest and fear, the flames of which were being fanned higher and higher until the climactic outburst in 1941. The proposal, however, was not given much support, the Dominion government disallowing such acts lest they should damage relations between Japan and Canada. But an early legislative attempt that did succeed was the 1895 extension of the provincial election act clause which deprived Chinese of the franchise to deprive the Japanese as well. It was to prove an important restriction.

Hostility continued to increase as the Japanese immigration question became increasingly difficult because in the last few years of the 19th century, the Japanese population began to increase rapidly. Mr. Carter-Cotton, provincial minister of finance and agriculture, pointed out, in February 1899, "it is unquestionably in the interests of the Empire that the Pacific province of the Dominion should be occupied by a large and thoroughly British population, rather than by one in which the number of aliens largely predominated and many of the distinctive features of a settled British community were lacking". And the Royal Commission which had been appointed in September 1901, to investigate Oriental immigration in B.C., reported that the economic rivalry that existed between the Japanese and Occidental workers was "creating a feeling so pronounced and bitter among a large class of whites, as to endanger the peace and be a fruitful source of international irritation". It further pointed out that the Japanese controlled the boat-building industry and were engaged in lumbering, mining, railway work and to a more limited extent in other operations. Already, little attempt was being made by the British Columbians to understand the Japanese.

This influx in 1907 was partly a result of an American regulation prohibiting Japanese immigrants to Hawaii from securing passports to go to the mainland. Since it was no longer possible to get into the U.S. by way of Hawaii, immigrants then in the Islands turned to B.C. as an alternative. The S.S. Kumeric, for example, carried 1,177 Japanese immigrants in one voyage from Hawaii to Vancouver in that year. Most of them had heard rumours that Canada was full of rattle-snakes and offered low wages, but they reasoned that they could easily go over to the U.S. once they got on Canadian soil. The Kumeric passengers almost starved enroute when the crossing took several days longer than expected, and upon reaching Vancouver, so anxious were they to get off the ship that dock officials had to play hoses on them in order to disperse them. Some 800 spent the first night in Steveston huddled under old canvas in a cannery net warehouse.

The Kumeric immigrants formed only one of boat-loads of Japanese that continued to arrive; and as condemnation from press platform increased, the matter fermented into the angry rioting that broke out in Vancouver on September 7, 1907. The rumoured arrival of some 2,000 or more Chinese and Japanese in the city sparked the outbreak. W. J. Bowser, a rising Conservative, had drawn up the "Bowser Natal Act", based on the Australian language tests designed to exclude Orientals from that Dominion, but Lieutenant-Governor Dunsmuir had refused to sign it, though it had been passed by the Legislature.

A civic mass meeting in Vancouver was organized by the Asiatic Exclusion League, and a mass parade was to march from Cambie Street grounds to the city hall. Early in the morning some 2,000 poured out of Cambie Street grounds with banners flying, and by the time the procession reached Hastings Street, the mob had increased to 5,000. At the city hall where an effigy of Dunsmuir was burned, at least 8,000 men gathered around. Inflammatory speeches were made by the leaders, hotly-worded resolutions were passed attacking Dunsmuir and calling for the resignation of Premier McBride. Outside the city hall, impromptu orators climbed telephone poles to harangue the crowd. Some 15,000 then began to march towards Pender Street, Chinatown's "main" street.

A stone tossed through the window of a Chinese store started the action; and considerable damage was done in Chinatown. But in the Japanese quarter, the mob did not fare as well. Armed with knives, broken beer bottles, clubs, the hardy Japanese beat off the mob until it dispersed. The Japanese then formed patrols, and no rioter could dent this protective cordon. They were beaten back if they tried. Under these conditions the mob could do little and the trouble subsided. A Royal Commission, under W. L. Mackenzie King, investigated the riot and set the total amount of damages to be paid to the Japanese at $9,175.00.

The riot of 1907 resulted in the first concrete restriction of Japanese immigration. The political storm in Canada aroused by the riots continued. In Vancouver, Conservative party leader Robert Borden declared two weeks later, "B.C. must remain a white man's country . . ." In 1908, the first Gentlemen's Agreement was announced. Japan agreed to permit only four classes of people to emigrate to Canada: first, returning immigrants and their wives and children; secondly, emigrants specially engaged by Japanese residents in Canada for bona fide personal or domestic service; thirdly, labourers under specifically-worded contracts approved by the Canadian Government; and fourthly, immigrants brought in under contract by Japanese resident agricultural holders in Canada. A total annual quota of 400 persons was fixed for all but the first group. In 1924, the agreement was modified to reducing the quota to 150 persons; and in 1928, a further limitation was introduced to include the wives and children of Japanese residents in Canada within the quota limitation.

After 1907, then, the total volume of immigration was substantially limited, but an even more significant change took place in the character of this immigration. Prior to 1907 the movement to Canada had consisted mainly of adult males. But following the first Gentlemen's Agreement, the number of female arrivals exceeded that of male immigrants in almost every year up to 1940. There were few females in B.C. before 1907. The first one, Mrs. Washiji Oya, landed in 1887 at Vancouver. Mrs. Naka Sekine, who came to Canada in 1890 when 14 years old, was another early arrival. Indeed, Mrs. Sekine was one of the longest to reside in Canada, for she died in March, 1958, in Hamilton, Ontario, at the age of eighty-two. But these, and a few other women, were exceptions. In 1901, in the over 4,000 Japanese in Canada, nearly all were male; but by 1921 there were 10,500 males and 5,300 females, and of the total number, 4,300 were children born in Canada. By 1931, these figures changed to 13,000 males and 9,200 females.

The Japanese problem still festered despite these agreements. For example, in the autumn of 1908 in B.C., one of the chief issues of the federal general election was Oriental immigration. Conservative party candidates made capital of the unrest in B.C. by making a special bid for anti-Oriental votes with a "White Canada" slogan, and the election resulted in a severe reverse to the Liberal party in the province. Indeed, agitation for the exclusion of the Japanese was part of the general anti-Oriental movement in B.C., and the movement became more intense during the depression years since 1929.

British Columbia MPs and MLAs also alleged that hundreds of Japanese were being smuggled into the country each year. But the Board of Review headed by Dr. H. L. Keenlyside which conducted extensive inquiries in 1938 reported that "it was generally agreed in official circles that very few Japanese had entered Canada illegally since 1932". After checking the allegations of illegal entry, the Board was convinced that these were without foundation.

One of the main reasons for the discontent in the province was the increase in native-born population. At first, migration of Japanese into Canada had been primarily of adult males, hoping for a quick and easy fortune. Thousands who came to Canada remained only briefly when they learned the actual conditions, but those who remained did so with serious intentions of permanent settlement. The immigration of the high percentage of women, and the establishment of family and home, meant that the movement now became one of immigrants arriving in B.C. with the intention of remaining, and perpetuating the continuing existence of the Japanese as a minority of importance in the life of the province.

2. Economic Expansion

Before 1941, over three fourths of the Japanese settlers in B.C. were clustered within 75 miles of Vancouver. The vast majority were in the city of Vancouver, in the villages of the Fraser Valley, and the coast of Vancouver Island. Vancouver alone had over 8,000 of the 22,205 Japanese in the province. The majority of the remaining Japanese settled down in the Okanagan Valley, and along the fishing and lumbering centres on the mainland coast. It was this high degree of concentration in certain areas that led critics to point out that it was evidence of a sinister central control of their activities. Together with their rapid economic expansion, this contributed greatly to the stormy history of the Japanese.

The rapidity of their expansion into the economic life of the province can be seen when one notes that in 1893 they were in six occupations; four decades later, these occupations had enlarged to over 60. In the early years, the Japanese were occupied in the major industries such as lumbering, fishing, mining, and railroading; but they gradually moved out of these industries into farming and occupations of a commercial nature, such as the proprietorship of stores and restaurants, and businesses and professions. This shift occurred mostly in the twenties when general expansion came to an end in these major industries. Also, the restrictions against the Japanese in these industries, and their search for better living conditions and a higher social status in the community made them seek occupations in which they could exercise a greater measure of independence.

By 1931, then, the Japanese had entered every industry, and most of the occupations in the province. One critic, for example, wrote: "The Japanese produce most of the strawberries, and about half of the raspberries. . . The situation is steadily growing worse, but it is when one looks into the future that its true seriousness is most apparent".

The case histories of hundreds of Japanese families follows a fairly common pattern. First, the Japanese entered the economic life of the province as unskilled laborers, floating from job to job, receiving the lowest wages. Then, as they gained skill and knowledge, they were able to command higher wages and accumulate capital. This was followed by an initial investment in some kind of productive resources--such as small farms, urban mercantile or service businesses . . . and establishment of permanent homes. Their struggle for status, and the discrimination to which it gave rise, made them branch out into new fields, particularly that of agriculture. In general, the story is that of an upward struggle for economic stability or self-sufficiency--an economic independence offering in some degree protection from discrimination and the vagaries of employers.

Ever since they immigrated to Canada, the Japanese have been associated with fishing. The fishing village of Steveston, for example, by the turn of the century had about 2,000 Japanese. And later they were to be found on all the important fishing areas of the coast--from the Fraser River up to the northern boundary of the province. Bringing valuable experience from the homeland where many had been fishermen under Fujiyama's shadow, the Japanese were an important factor in the development of this industry in B.C.

The fishing industry soon became the scene of an acute struggle for supremacy in the competition between the Japanese and the Occidentals and Indians. By 1901 the Japanese held over 2,000 fishing licenses, and it was estimated that over 4,000 Japanese were engaged in this industry. Indeed, complaints were made that they were driving others out of the industry; and, as a result, successful attempts to reduce licenses to the Japanese were made during the twenties so that by the period just before World War II, less than 15% of tht total number of licenses were held by the Japanese. Nonetheless, they continued to be an important factor in fish production. Then, too, they were credited with the development of herring and dog salmon fishing, salt herring industries, and developing new markets for fish in the Orient.

Lumbering also has been closely associated with the Japanese. The more important communities where they were employed were Vancouver, New Westminster, Fraser Mills, Mission City, Woodfibre, Ocean Falls, Port Alice, Alberni, Royston, Fanny Bay and Courtenay. In Ocean Falls, for example, Japanese Laborers held in the clearing of land for the first sawmill in 1906. By 1900 they were in all branches of lumbering; again, this situation evoked the animosity of the white laborers. Every effort was made to drive them out of the industry; operators on provincial lands were threatened with the loss of their licenses if they employed Japanese, and Japanese operators were unable to retain their licenses or get new ones in the period just before World War I.

As in the fishing industry, restrictions were made against the Japanese until the numbers of those engaged in lumbering showed a serious decline. Yet some of the forest workers eventually became fairly large logging operators, and by 1933 there were some fourteen such operators in the province. The others continued to work as wage-earners in Vancouver or the company towns on the mainland and on Vancouver Island.

By 1941, agriculture came to be the most important occupational endeavour of the Japanese. A great number of the immigrants had originally been farmers in Japan, and once they had accumulated enough capital, they bought or leased small farm lands. Also, they turned to farming because in other industries restrictions and agitations made it difficult to secure a livelihood with any degree of security.

Since they had only limited resources, they were unable to acquire developed farms in well-settled areas. They therefore took up uncleared lands and developed them into fertile farms of high productivity. Pioneering in the bushlands, they built up a thriving industry. Through hard work, irrigation, and perseverance, hundreds of acres of tomatoes, berries, and other vegetables and fruits grew in the Fraser Valley. On the shores of the Okanagan, apples and pears glistened in the sunlight. Lord Aberdeen's Coldstream Ranch in Vernon was the scene in the early 1900's where many Japanese learned the art of fruit farming. In 1927, for example, it was estimated that the total agricultural acreage owned by Japanese in B.C. amounted to almost 10,000 acres valued at $1,252,063.00. The greater number were engaged in mixed farming or soft fruit growing. Indeed, in berry growing, which was the chief branch of agriculture in which they engaged, they came to assume the dominant position among farmers. A secondary concentration occurred in the greenhouse industry, while individual operators built up important and substantial poultry farms, market gardens and nurseries.

The Japanese were also prominent in two major industries: mining and railroad construction. From the early nineties on, Japanese laborers were brought to work in mines under contract basis, until agitation eliminated further importation, and the number of workers steadily declined. They entered the railroading industry as early as 1899, and in 1907 the CPR contracted to import 1,000 laborers, though only 370 were actually brought because of protests. But just as in mining, the number of workers declined until it became negligible.

The early immigrants had looked for employment in the basic industries, but soon there was a trend towards settling into urban communities where they started modest retail and service establishments, especially in Vancouver. Again, as the majority of Japanese settled in one part of the province, so too in Vancouver, the majority tended to concentrate in three of four districts. "Little Tokyo", the main district, came to be located on the eastern outskirts of the business centre of the city. The principal thoroughfare was Powell Street, between Main and Campbell Streets, where they were located, the commercial enterprises and community gathering places. But as more came to be able to afford it, they began a slight exodus into the better residential areas of the city.

In 1931, when the Japanese in Vancouver totalled 8,328, there were 858 trade licenses issued to Japanese; in other words, a license was issued to one out of every ten Japanese, whereas there was only one for every 21 non-Orientals. Consequently, there was talk of restricting the number of such licenses to the Japanese.

Thus the immigrants had started at the very bottom of the Canadian economic ladder--as section workers on the railroads, domestics in the homes of the well-to-do, hired hands on farms. But by years of hard work and frugal living, they had acquired a stake in the land, ownership of their own fishing boats and equipment, or a small business in the cities, and a few had risen to positions of prominence and wealth.

3. The Rising Tide of Discrimination

Up to the years before 1941, then, the Japanese Canadians in general had become established economically, and the future held some hope despite the hostility that surrounded them. Immigration, too, had virtually ceased; the numbers still arriving were just a trickle. But life for the Japanese was a continuous struggle for a better standard of living and a higher social status. This naturally involved them in contact with the Occidental population. And their history evolved into a continual struggle to survive against the odds of discrimination.

The contacts of the Japanese with the Occidentals were virtually confined to the occupations in which they worked together. And when competition existed, the result was conflict. This conflict broke out into the open with such incidents as the 1907 riot, flared up after World War I when returning veterans found their jobs occupied by the Japanese, and gradually spread out from the few industries in which it arose. Public sentiment, too, became swayed by the grievances and accusations of the small minority of Occidentals who met and dealt with the Japanese in occupational situations.

Organized labor, in the early years, agitated strenuously against the admission of Japanese immigrants because they enjoyed unrestricted competition in the major industries. But later, labor realized that the solution to the problem was to invite the Japanese to become partners in its fight for higher wages and a shorter working week. They hoped to reduce their advantage in competition by raising the standard of living. The early antagonistic role of organized labor, however, was quickly filled by others, such as the farmers, fishermen and small business men who bore the brunt of competition as the Japanese gradually moved out of the class of laborers and assumed proprietorship, owning their own fishing boats, farms, and small businesses.

Nothing short of wholesale discrimination seemed to be the object of the agitators. The White Canada Association became the most militant of the groups together with such patriotic organizations as the Native Sons of B.C. and Native Sons of Canada. They were among a long line of similar organizations which played a prominent part of the anti-Japanese sentiment in the province. From the early days until after World War II, the province was never without at least one of these zealous groups which agitated against the Japanese. There were, of course, groups which sympathized with the Japanese. These included the financial and industrial leaders of the province who were friendly to the Japanese, mainly because of their commercial interests in the Orient, and a small group of educators and clergymen. The agitators, however, were the more vocal and aggressive group.

In 1902, the Legislature of B.C. passed a measure disenfranchising British citizens of Asiatic origin in the province of B.C. Those born in Canada and Japanese from Japan alike ceased to have the right to vote in B.C., though they could vote in the other provinces. Even those veterans who served in the Canadian Expeditionary Force in France (197 Japanese enlisted, of whom 54 were killed in action) were not granted permission to vote provincially or federally in B.C. until 1931. And only by a margin of one vote did the provincial legislature allow this exception.

What did this disenfranchisement mean? It meant exclusion from a whole series of activities in the political and economic life of the province. The Japanese Canadians could not become candidates for election to the Legislature, municipal councils, or the school boards; they could not vote in federal or municipal elections. Also, exclusion from the voters' list made them ineligible for certain professions such as pharmacy and law.

The Vancouver Province stated editorially in September, 1940:
"Though of an alien race, they are our people. They are Canadians . . . The main trouble in B.C. is that those Canadian-born people are refused the provincial franchise--which automatically also deprives them of Dominion franchise. Thus they have no votes. If they could vote, they would be treated fairly by politicians; they could protect themselves in a measure. As it is, they are at the mercy of any demagogue who wants to make capital out of prejudice against the Japanese".

Then, too, there were other restrictions against their earning a living. They were excluded by law from employment on timber leases, from obtaining licenses as hand loggers, from employment by a Government contractor. It was a general policy to exclude them from employment in provincial or municipal services or as school teachers. And a large number of Japanese had been eliminated from the fishing industry by reduction in the number of licenses granted to the Japanese. And so it went on. These restrictions presented a kind of legacy to the children of the immigrants born in Canada.

Then there were the occasional outbreaks of physical violence. In the Hallowe'en celebration of 1939, for example, a mob of some 300 Occidental youths invaded the Japanese shopping district on Powell Street, and caused several hundreds of dollars' damage to property. They smashed plate glass windows and looted stores, before a call to police headquarters brought sufficient officers to disperse the mob.

The Japanese, probably more than any other immigrant group in Canada, took full advantage of the educational institutions. They were very eager to give their children an education. Many of the second generation (the Nisei) went on to the more advanced schools; and the percentage of Nisei who entered university was not much below the percentage for the whole province, which was remarkable considering the economic standing of the parents. In the years 1916 - 1939, 55 Japanese students graduated from the University of British Columbia, entering into many fields. In scholarship, the second generation were considered generally equal, if not superior, to other school children. Then, too, their juvenile delinquency rates were conspicuously lower than those of other groups. Indeed, statistics have shown that the Japanese were among the most law-abiding citizens in the country.

Much criticism had been levied against the presence of Japanese language schools in which reading, writing, dictation and composition were taught for about two hours daily. Critics pointed out that they conflicted with the programme of the public schools, taxed the strength and injured the health of the children. They also resented the existence of the language schools as an indication of the natural loyalty to Japanese culture by adult members. But to the parents, the language school was a means by which they might lessen the distance between themselves and their children. They also felt that ability to read and write Japanese was a necessary adjunct because racial discrimination lessened job opportunities in the open market. As the international situation became more acute, however, the school issue was often used as a means of stirring up suspicion.

Life for the adolescent Nisei was pleasant enough in the schools where they cultivated friendships and won respect, but after high school, it became a succession of closing doors. Bewildering incidents such as segregation in theatres, and exclusion from public places such as the Crystal Pool in Vancouver, were commonplace. But despite the closing wedge of unfriendliness, the Nisei lived to a large extent like their white contemporaries. In music, sports, literature, and amusements, their interests were predominantly Western rather than Japanese.

It was when they began to seek employment that the full brunt of animosity was felt. Discriminatory measures, especially in occupational activities, were levied against them, though they were born in Canada. Educated in the schools of the province, brought up in its churches, denied the right to vote, they were aliens in the land of their birth, citizens without the basic rights of citizenship. Free social intercourse was closed to them because of economic differences which in turn were caused by inequality of vocational opportunities. As the Nisei were so limited in the field of employment, they often found themselves engaged in work with other Japanese, and consequently their personal daily contacts were largely confined to members of their own group. But through perseverance the Nisei hoped to gain acceptance and their rights as citizens. With restrictions barring his path on every hand, either because of popular feeling or because of law, the average Japanese found only a few lines of economic activity open to him. And these lines, practically without exception, were the least lucrative, the least promising, the most despised lines of economic servitude. For the Japanese Canadians, there existed no comfortable and lucrative jobs.

4. The Society

Like any other immigrant group, the Japanese partook of two worlds: the one which he shared with his fellow immigrants because it was a link with their past in Japan, and the other which he had in common with the other groups in the Canadian community. Then, too, there came to be a tremendous difference between the generation born in Canada (the Nisei) and the first generation of immigrants (the Issei), as the former came to be rapidly assimilated in the ways of the larger community.

Japanese Canadian society in the period before World War II was generally determined by the patterns of behaviour brought to Canada from Japan. Foremost of the ties were those associated with the family as the basic social unit. In brief, it was this: the men were looked upon as the backbone of the family, with the father as the supreme authority; the women were in the position of complete obedience as were the children; and the selection of mates was controlled by the parents. This was the traditional pattern. So naturally there were conflicts as the children born and educated in Canada grew up, and rebelled against this rigid authoritarian system. It differed in almost every respect with the typical Anglo Saxon ideas of the family unit.

The break between the two generations, Issei and Nisei, tended to get wider as the Japanese became more settled. The children went to school, learned English, and acquired Western habits and cultural traits--different from those their parents knew. Most of the Issei felt themselves unable to change or reconcile themselves to the change in the Nisei as the latter grew to become more and more independent. Yet, the second generation, compared with other children in the communities in which they lived, were thought to be models of propriety. Although becoming more assimilated, they still displayed the qualities of perseverance and industriousness which enabled their parents to succeed. In the educational institutions of the province, for example, the Nisei made enviable reputations for themselves.

But the lot of the second generation was not entirely happy. On the one hand, they were criticized by their parents for adopting the habits of the Occidentals--they were accused of lacking industry and thrift and determination; on the other hand, they were attacked by Occidentals because they retained the physical characteristics of their parents. The lot of the second generation was bewildering. As the products of Japanese culture, the parents remained devoted to the old system; the children, on the other hand, became advocates of the new. This, no doubt would be true of any immigrant group, but in the case of the Japanese, the issues were more pronounced because of the provincial discrimination and restrictions practised against them.

The majority of the immigrants were Buddhists, but the development of an organized Church was slow, particularly because of the antagonism of Occidentals who felt it was another manifestation of Japanese imperialism. The first Buddhist temple was opened in Vancouver in 1905, and a priest brought over from Japan. In 1934, the Buddhist Church in B.C. consisted of five missions and six branches, with a total membership of about 1,500. And though the organization of the Church improved, the hold of Buddhism greatly declined, though nominally it was the largest group with 14,707 being listed as Buddhists.

Christianity, on the other hand, experienced unusual progress in the first four decades since the Japanese first settled. In 1931, there were 7,239 Japanese Christians in the province, almost one-third of the total population, with the United Church of Canada the most popular Christian denomination. One of the reasons for conversion to Christianity was the fact that the Christian Church was the first, and perhaps the only, important institution that aided the Japanese in the early years.

One of the remarkable growths among the communities was the development of organizations; in 1934, there were about 230 units of religious and secular organizations, 84 of them in Vancouver alone. Indeed, the Vancouver community was in nearly all respects the focal centre of all the communities in the province, the centre of activity and influence. These were such groups as the "ken-jin-kai" or prefectural associations, whose membership was made up of immigrants from the same prefecture or province in Japan. Then, too, there were many specialized groups such as trade associations, barbers, rooming house proprietors, gardeners, dry cleaners, etc., as well as educational, cultural, and political groups. One of the most influential was the Canadian Japanese Association, organized in 1897, which aided many immigrants to find positions, learn English, maintain a high moral standard, encouraged immigrants to become naturalized, and combatted discrimination. The CJA, which claimed to represent the entire Japanese community, had a pronounced nationalistic basis, having close associations with the Japanese consulate. Its leadership was in the hands of the more wealthy businessmen. The Camp and Mill Workers' Union, which presented a challenge to the CJA's authority and prestige, advocated co-operation with the Occidentals, rather than the separatist tendencies of the CJA. Its leaders represented a bloc of younger Issei, some with a broader education and a white-collar background. It was organized in 1920 for the purpose of promoting trade unionism among Japanese, and attempted to educate immigrants to Western standards and customs. Thus it believed that the future of the Japanese in Canada depended upon co-operation with Occidentals and that prejudice could be overcome by a positive approach. In 1931, it was instrumental in having the Trades and Labor Congress of Canada endorse the request of the Nisei for "equality of treatment and full rights of citizenship". It even published a daily newspaper in Japanese, one of the three vernacular dailies in Vancouver.

In some of the small communities, the trade organizations, such as fishermen's associations, served to protect the occupational interests of their members, combat restrictions, and function generally in the interest of the Japanese community, giving financial and moral guidance and leadership. To the suspicious however, these organizations gave rise to the belief that they were under some kind of central control, that some kind of national genius directed the "peaceful penetration" into Canada of people of Japanese descent.

Up to 1941, the first generation immigrants still dominated the community to a large extent. But for ten years, the ferment of independence had been brewing within the Canadian-born second generation. The challenge to traditional community authority had reached by the time of World War II, the stage of scarcely disguised defiance. The Nisei citizenship movement culminated in the Japanese Canadian Citizens League, organized in spring of 1936, with chapters located in various parts of the province. The JCCL was in essence the institutionalized medium of a political rebellion. It was the first organized stage in the evolution of the second generation who had come to realize their unique status in the national life of Canada. The JCCL made repeated attempts to secure the united support of all Nisei organizations, tried to provide for the social requirements of the second generation, attempted to aid in development of new Leaders through the sponsorship of oratorical and essay contests, and held forums to provide open discussion of various problems. They took part in various congresses of youth groups and took every possible opportunity to interpret the aims and aspirations of the Japanese Canadians to the public.

Thus since about 1930, the change in community structure was taking place with the emergence of the second generation as a growing voice in the community. And by the time the evacuation came in 1942, the shift from the dominance of the old generation to the new was well under way. The second generation began about the mid-thirties to appeal vigorously for the removal of discriminatory restrictions, the right to vote; in short, to be given the rights of Canadian citizenship. In 1936, a delegation appeared in Ottawa before the Special Committee on Elections and Franchise Acts of the House of Commons to request a revision of the legislation which prevented them from voting. This was the beginning of their formal agitation for the franchise.

An important event in this shift was the publication of The New Canadian, which first appeared on November, 1938, and was the only newspaper to continue publishing through the wartime period. The newspaper, through the efforts of editor Thomas Shoyama who guided it through most of the trying years, continually agitated for unconditional acceptance in Canadian life for Japanese Canadians and provided an organ for the articulate members of the second generation to voice their opinions not only to their own group but to the Canadian public at large. The Nisei, too, were beginning a period of self-scrutiny: a few were looking to resettlement in the eastern provinces for better economic and social opportunities; others advocated the assumption of pioneering in the whole field of human relationships by meeting the hard facts of life and trying to overcome them.

Life in the Powell Streets of B.C. cannot really be relegated to a set of statistics, nor did it consist of sombre incidents alone. There was laughter, too, though behind it was inescapably the hint of tears; their life was shot through with sunlight and shadow. There were idle, carefree chatter, friendly happy faces, the sound of merry tunes, the echoing noise of ball on bat, the strange mingled smell of burnt toast and sukiyaki. The Powell Streets were much more than streets; they were, as one of their young poets put it, their main streets, dream streets, park avenues, wall streets, and for the second generation they were "the nucleus of a grander scheme", a brave new world to come.

II PEARL HARBOUR AND EVACUATION

1. The Established Notions

Then came December 7, 1941, when the bombs fell at Pearl Harbour and sundered the Canadian and Japanese nations violently apart. The 20,000 Japanese Canadians became helpless victims as tensions and prejudices flared up in the Pacific coast province.

There had been many charges hurled against the Japanese in the years when the prospect of the war spreading to the Pacific area loomed large. So acute was the war agitation that late in 1940 the federal government had undertaken to ease the situation by appointment of a special committee of inquiry. In January, 1941, Prime Minister Mackenzie King tabled the report of the Committee which urged the importance of checking irresponsible attacks upon the Japanese in B.C. as "an integral part of civil security and national defense". It was also announced that a special registration of all persons of Japanese ancestry would be immediately undertaken by the federal police as a key supervisory measure. It is noteworthy that the Prime Minister agreed with the Committee's report:

> "After careful study of the entire question, it is the opinion of the committee, and in this the government fully shares, that the most serious danger in the B.C. situation is that arising from ill-informed attacks against the loyalty and integrity of the Oriental population".

Before Pearl Harbour, there had long been a fear of invasion of the coast, and there had also been a long established desire to expel the Japanese Canadians from the province forever. Pearl Harbour created the immediate possibility of the first, and gave an opportunity for the second. What followed December 7, 1941, was the complete disruption of the Japanese Canadians from their normal tenor of living: a programme of complete evacuation, resettlement, and an attempt at deportation.

Even before Pearl Harbour, the people of the province had been persuaded to look on the Japanese Canadian residents as a menace. Almost every conceivable device was used to create a mounting impression that all people of Japanese ancestry were sly, sinister, unprincipled, biologically more fertile than the white man, and incapable of loyalty to Canada.

One of the major charges levied against the Japanese was that they were satisfied with a low standard of living and thus were disinclined to become Canadians in the full sense of the word. The agitators looked at the rundown Powell Street settlement of Vancouver and the fishing village of Steveston, and decided that the Japanese were a threat because of a low standard of living. Yet, it was attributable to racial discrimination that the Japanese were forced to remain in such conditions: people were not eager to sell or rent to Japanese Canadians in the better areas, legislation also made it difficult for them to raise their standards of living and occupations. Then, too, many Japanese had improved their homes; the group as a whole was blamed for the more conspicuous poorer ones.

The "inassimilability" of the Japanese was another well-worn theme; it was presented as enough reason to send all Japanese Canadians to Japan. A low standard of living, the existence of Japanese language schools, the self-sufficient communities--all these, and more, seemed to the agitators to be enough reason. The catch phrase, "peaceful penetration", was also aired, pointing attention to what was thought of as an insidious infiltration into Canada by the Japanese immigrants. In short, the agitators felt that all activities were controlled by the Government of Japan; for example, that Japanese fishing was an attempt to learn and occupy strategic positions for eventual military operations. It was a thoroughly digest notion that the fishermen could not be trusted. Another was that the Japanese government supplied the capital for the establishment of businesses. Agitators could not, nor did want to, distinguish between the people of Japan and the Japanese Canadians. Some extremists had political careers resting in a large degree upon their opposition to the Japanese.

The dawn attack on Pearl Harbour could only precipitate these and other established notions which had been nurtured for such a long time. If there ever was a chance to realize the wish of ridding the province entirely of its Japanese, this was it. Only a small minority of individuals and groups, such as the Vancouver Consultative Council and the CCF Party, which lost many a vote by its stand, tried to understand the situation rationally. An incredible network of organized propaganda by interests willing to use any bludgeon to gain their ends had been in existence, and sprang into action.

One incident demonstrates the tactics used. Long before the war, in 1937, the brother of the Emperor, Prince Chichibu, had visited Vancouver. After his departure The Vancouver Sun received a letter, signed with five Japanese names, protesting that this city had not shown proper respect for the Prince. Needless to say, it roused the anger of the city. A group of Nisei were convinced that the letter was bogus, written only to arouse feeling against the Japanese community. They investigated, found that no Japanese existed with the names on the letter, and reported to the Sun which

readily agreed that the letter was a fake. Yet after the wartime
agitation began, this letter was dramatically used by apparently
reputable interests and reported in the Sun, to show that the
Japanese had close and mysterious links with Japan. And those
interests knew that the letter was a fabrication. Lacking the
franchise, and with the attack led by politically important groups,
the Japanese Canadians became victimized in the succession of
events that followed.

2. <u>Pressure and Policy</u>

The Japanese, foreign-born and native-born alike, were
reregistered on a voluntary basis by the Standing Committee on
Orientals in January, 1941, but after Pearl Harbour this was made
compulsory. This was the first in a series of official acts which
set aside privileges of citizenship. Letters to the editor of British
Columbia newspapers urged, increasingly, that all Japanese be
removed and held in detention; no effort was made to discriminate
between citizen or non-citizen, loyal or disloyal. Cooler heads
suggested that consideration be given to them, but the pressure of
ingrained hostility fermented by war-produced emotionalism soon
prompted the evacuation.

The advent of war meant more to the Japanese than any
other single group in Canada, for they were caught between their
feelings of loyalty to Canada and the distrust of the Occidentals who
would not let them be Canadians. The New Canadian immediately
after Pearl Harbour stated editorially:

"There must be now, just as there has been in the
past, complete, unswerving loyalty to the country
that has given us birth, protection and sustenance...
This tragic conflict will set back, but it must not
destroy our hopes and aspirations to walk with
honour and with equality as Canadians among all
Canadians".

In spite of it all, among the people "there is an air of confidence,
a continuing belief that they need not despair". But it was not to
be.

This "air of confidence" was destroyed in the swift
weeks that followed as the Japanese were branded as "enemy aliens".
Few British Columbians had reduced the question of defense to a
purely rational basis, where they could distinguish between resident
immigrant Japanese and those now become enemies. Unemployment
faced the Japanese on large scale, and day-to-day routine became
upside down. Rocks were thrown through some grocery store
windows, saw mill hands were laid off in Vancouver, arson was
attempted at one rooming house on Alexandra Street. A mingled

fear and strain settled over Powell Street and all the other
communities in the province.

There was little doubt that the Pacific Coast was
suffering from the worst attack of war nerves in its history. And
the Japanese community, which was attacked so flagrantly even in
times of peace, was taking the worst beating since the riots of 1907.
Fishing boats were impounded, and later brought down under naval
escort from Steveston, Nanaimo, the upper Fraser, the gulf islands,
and up coast, to be anchored at the New Westminster breakwater.
Eighteen hundred fishermen, their wives, and children were affected.
Some vessels were sunk after clumsy collisions in the heavy seas
and fog, others allowed to drift up on the beach, and many delicately
tuned engines were mishandled so that they were practically ruined.

There were a few weeks of relative calm immediately
after Pearl Harbour, but by the end of the year, Members of
Parliament from B.C., local Conservative and Liberal Associations,
City and District Councils, labour unions, veterans associations,
and community service groups, all moved towards demanding the
removal of all Japanese "east of the rockies". Alderman Halford
Wilson of Vancouver was one of the most vociferous in the crescendo
of demands. Thomas Reid, who with other MP's such as Ian
Mackenzie, A. W. Neill and Howard Green, were among the most
outspoken anti-Japanese political leaders, told the East Burnaby
Liberal Association on January 15, 1942:

> "Take them back to Japan. They do not belong here
> and there is only one solution to the problem. They
> cannot be assimilated as Canadians for no matter how
> long the Japanese remain in Canada they will always
> be Japanese".

In the interior cities such as Vernon, Kamloops and Kelowna, anti-
Japanese agitation was also moving quickly in time and tempo with
that of the coast. All of these individuals and groups, then, kept
up a sustained drive for eleven weeks, until Mackenzie King's
announcement of complete evacuation on February 26, 1942.
Spring was an impossible dream for the Japanese Canadians.

Thus the wholesale evacuation was never conceived as a
conscious policy from the beginning by the Federal Government;
rather it was forced upon the government by pressure from B.C.
The initials action of the Government was basically of a precautionary
nature. Some forty Japanese nationals allegedly dangerous to the
security of the state, were detained on December 8, 1941, under the
Defense of Canada regulations, most of whom were cleared and
released from custody within a year's time. Under advisement of
police, the 59 Japanese language schools and three vernacular
newspapers closed down voluntarily to avoid, as the RCMP put it,
"misunderstandings or ill-feelings on the part of the whites who might
resent the existence of newspapers printed in the language of the enemy".

On January 14, 1942, partial evacuation was announced. A "protected area" was established from which "all enemy aliens" would be excluded. Strict surveillance of all Japanese nationals was to be continued, with prohibitions on use of short-wave radios and cameras. It was proposed that the exclusion of Japanese Canadians from the Armed Forces should be continued. And on February 5, 1942, the Minister of Justice ordered all male enemy aliens of 18 to 45 years to leave the protected coastal area, before April 1. The "protected area" was a narrow 100 mile wide strip bounded on one side by the Pacific Ocean, the other by the Cascade Range, reaching from Alaska and ending at the U.S. border. It contained practically all the Japanese communities in the province. The first contingent of 100 Japanese male nationals left Vancouver to disembark February 24 at Rainbow and Lucerne, B.C., deep in the snows of the Canadian Rockies--the vanguard of some 1,700 male nationals who were to be removed from the coast and placed on federal road projects for the duration.

But this moderate policy was a failure as pressure and impatience over the inaction of the Government increased. Singapore, after all, had fallen on February 15. In quick order, a whole series of repressive measures, unlike anything before in the history of the nation, were authorized. The new orders, in effect, uprooted completely some 20,000 men, women and children, and reduced to nothing the concept and value of Canadian citizenship. On February 26, Orders-in-Council announced that all prohibitions with regard to a number of special articles such as radios and cameras, and automobiles were extended to Canadian citizens of Japanese descent in B.C. as well. RCMP officers were authorized to search without warrant any house or premise and to seize any of the special articles. A curfew regulation was introduced confining everyone to their homes between sunset and sunrise. And finally, every person of Japanese race, citizen and alien, was ordered "to leave the protected area forthwith". These were restrictions amounting in sum to a practical application of martial law.

3.   The Removal

The rules of a shattered world crumbled faster and closer around 20,000 bewildered people in the first week of March, as governmental machinery moved on with its work. By early spring of 1942, the 20,000 Japanese had reached what was probably the lowest status that any group of comparable size had ever experienced. They had been removed from their homes by governmental fist. They had lost all freedom of movement and practically all opportunities of engaging in private employment and earning anything more than a subsistance livelihood. Jobs of long years' standing had gone, businesses and homes, farms and stores, built up with years of toil were gone. The fruit of struggle and labour, that an aging generation had hoped to enjoy in its old age, was snatched away. The hopes and ambitions of a rising generation of Canadians were dashed to the ground. Family ties, between husband and wife, father and children, brother and sister, were torn apart. The Japanese were a lonely crowd, hemmed in by the masses of indifferent or hostile Canadians, with only a handful of people believing in them.

That there was no evidence, based upon military information or upon the practical results of measures already taken, which justified the removal of the Japanese, was ignored. On March 4, the B.C. Security Commission was created for carrying out the tasks of removal. Punishment of any person contravening or failing to comply with the regulations was set: maximum fine of $500.00 or a prison term of twelve months. Six months in jail with hard labour was the sentence imposed by a Vancouver magistrate on Sotaro Saki, 66, who was found violating curfew. The Commission, on the basis of the War Measures Act, had been given complete authority to regulate completely the life of all Japanese, regardless of citizenship.

The actual evacuation took nine months, from early February through October of 1942. The first stage for those living outside Vancouver was from their homes to Hastings Park Clearing Station, and the second from the Park to interior B.C. Two buildings used for the annual exhibitions, the Women's Building and the Livestock Building, were leased for four months. Both of these buildings underwent almost complete renovation as civilian workers and soldiers installed wash basins, toilets and baths. And a new experience in communal living began for the evacuees.

At the peak of its population, on September 1, there were 3,866 in the Park, and though people left for interior points each day since the first evacuees entered the Park on March 16, it was not until September that large numbers were evacuated daily. Also, some families went directly to the sugar beet projects in Alberta or to other employment, and the majority of the Vancouver residents were moved directly to interior points.

There was great confusion and disorder both in the orders and the carrying out of the first stages of evacuation. Some people living in remote places received as little as 24 hours' notice. One resident of Hyde Creek could do nothing with his household and real property because he was given only two hours' notice to vacate. Persons in Cumberland were given a week's notice to move to Hastings Park, and were told that one suitcase and one clothes bag were the only baggage allowed. This situation was repeated in numerous cases; many people departed with only the barest necessities and could make no arrangements for the care of property or household goods because of the precipitate nature of the evacuation.

A report published by the B.C. Security Commission on April 6, 1942, stated 20,000 would be moved to one of four projects:

male nationals chiefly to roadwork on the province; the majority of the second generation to Ontario roads or industry; farming and fishing families to Southern Alberta and Manitoba; thousands of women and children to "ghost towns in the interior". Evacuation of Canadian-born males of Japanese origin out of the protected area had gotten underway on March 27, 1942, when 133 men left for Schreiber, Ontario. But husbands and fathers were loathe to leave for work elsewhere since they had no definite knowledge as to what would happen to their families.

It was expected at first that 4,000 men would be moved to road camps to work on the miles of new highways that the province needed so badly to join inland areas to the coast. The Japanese would provide cheap labor, and it would be possible to keep them under strict guard. And since many communities and provincial governments indicated that they did not want the Japanese to be moved into their regions, it was thought that sending the males to road camps and the women and children to ghost towns would solve the problem. But cheap rates of pay--a basic 25 cents an hour rate with deductions of $22.50 for board, and in the case of a married man, a deduction of $20.00 for the family,--meant that a pittance of $7.50 would remain per month for clothing and incidentals. Insecurity, separation from family, anxiety over the disposition of property at home, harassed the men.

But many of the 26 different road projects which the Security Commission listed were located where there was possibility of sabotage; consequently, the Department of National Defense objected. Also, a number of men objected to going such a long way to places such as Schreiber, Ontario, and thus become separated from families. These difficulties, therefore, made the Commission revise its policy slightly, and make plans for all married men to rejoin their families "before winter" of 1942.

Family groups at this time also moved to sugar beet growing areas of Alberta, Manitoba and Ontario. These agricultural areas took on new importance during the war when sugar became scarce, and such a project allowed the Japanese to be moved in family groups. Thus by June 25, 1942, beet projects had taken 3,879 persons from B.C.'s "protected area".

4.   The Ghost Towns

Settling down in the ghost towns of southeastern B.C. in the Kootenay Lake and Slocan Valley areas--Greenwood, Slocan City, New Denver, Kaslo, Roseberry, Sandon, Lemon Creek,--plus the Hope, B.C. centre, and Tashme, was marked by confusion and hardships for the 11,964 evacuees. These towns were former mining towns renovated to receive the influx of evacuees, and, in the case of Tashme, a newly constructed camp. Ghost towns partially solved

the problem of the shortage of construction supplies; the movement
of evacuees would also stimulate business for local residents. But
the houses, whether renovated or newly built units, were mostly
congested. Small hotel rooms, about 12 by 14 feet, sometimes housed
as many as seven occupants. Most of the "new" houses were hastily
built, tar-papered three-room frame structures. In the early
months, some of the men in the Slocan project even lived in tents.
A semblance of normal domestic life had to be hewn out of crude
surroundings. Families had to adapt themselves to the routine of
lamps and candles, water from outside taps, double-decker beds,
community baths, and primitive sewage facilities. And it was a
long time before electricity, sewage and running water taps were
installed in some of the towns.

For most of the evacuees who had lived for years in the
temperate coastal climates, the heavy cold and snow of the first
winter proved to be a hardship, especially as the houses and the
green firwood hardly provided protection against the elements.
Congestion also meant that families had to share cooking facilities;
as many as fourteen families had to share one large stove in some of
the old hotels. Most of these evacuee centres afforded lovely vistas:
Slocan City, for example, was nestled beside a lake, sheltered by
mountains, and full of houses that were relics of a romantic and
flamboyant past. Indeed, a sense of the past made itself felt in
these ghost towns with their old hotels and buildings, the exciting
days of the mining booms. But the evacuees were more conscious
of the delapidation, leaky roofs, rough slivered floors and frozen
water pipes.

Yet, because the Canadian government did not wish to
cause any international incident--or any reprisals by the Japanese
government on Canadians living in Japan or any of the conquered
areas--by having a Japanese Canadian die from medical neglect,
medical care and treatment were adequate in these interior settlements. The Jackson Royal Commission which investigated these
towns in March, 1944, stated that they were "reasonably adequate',
insofar as they were "temporary means of meeting an emergency".
But the Commission also confirmed the indictment of the provincial
government in refusing "to take any responsibility for the education"
of the children.

Indeed, in the matter of education for the evacuated
children, the provincial Department of Education evaded any kind of
responsibility. It refused to be liable for any part of the cost of
educating them. Thus the federal government had to assume the
task, though it was not until December, 1942, that the schools
became ready for operation. In the Bay Farm and Lemon Creek
centres in the Slocan Valley, they were not ready for 1,200 children
until April, 1943. In the self-supporting projects such as Christina
Lake, Minto, Bridge River, and East Lillooet, arrangements were
made with local school boards as few children were involved. But

in the case of the large centres, most of the children lost a year of education before the makeshift schools became ready. Even at that, the Security Commission arranged only for public school education; kindergarten and high school work were carried on by the churches, and correspondence courses in high school work had to be undertaken by the student at his own expense.

Providing sufficient and competent teachers was also a problem. In the settlements, there were only two trained teachers since a teaching career was not possible among the Japanese Canadians before the war. Thus the bulk of the teaching had to be done by volunteers among the ranks of university and high school graduates. But with poor facilities and environmental conditions, the system was not all that could have been desired. Most of the schools even lacked blackboards, an obvious necessity, as well as an adequate supply of textbooks. In Tashme, for example, the school was a barn divided into rooms by part-way partitions which created difficulties in terms of discipline and acoustics.

5. Nisei Enlistment

It was not until early in 1945 that the bars against Nisei enlistment in the Canadian army were lifted after five years of struggle against official discouragement. In the years before the war, the official policy of excluding Japanese from service was rooted in anti-Japanese feeling. After Canada made its historic declaration of war when Hitler let loose his legions upon Poland, a group of Nisei offered their service and pledged their loyalty in a telegram to Ottawa. It was not long before Nisei throughout scattered parts of the province were volunteering, only to be rejected.

New agitation was rising, too, about this time as the Rome-Berlin-Tokyo Axis began to assume clearer shape. And when the National Resources Mobilization Act became effective in the latter part of the summer of 1940, the question of service for Japanese Canadians became acute. A number of Nisei received official notices ordering them to report for medical check-up in connection with military service. Medicals were completed, but no calls came. The Vancouver City Council requested the Dominion Government not to call up the Japanese if it meant giving them the Dominion franchise. And in December, 1940, the special elections committee of the B.C. Legislature decided, despite opposition by CCF members, that Canadian-born Orientals, even though they served would not be entitled to vote at the next provincial election.

In January, 1941, Prime Minister King stated that in accordance with a recommendation of its investigating commission, it had been decided for the time being that Canadian-born Orientals would not be drafted. This decision was assailed by representatives of 25 Nisei groups, who asked for the same treatment accorded to all Canadians. This exemption had set the Japanese community further apart from the rest of the country.

The commission's report had declared emphatically that there was no evidence of disloyalty, and it denounced the racist campaign against the Japanese. It stated that hostility towards "the Japanese had been deliberately inflamed by certain individuals... for personal political advantage". But since the situation in B.C. might further be complicated by acts committed outside of Canada, these might provoke action against the Japanese, and if there were Japanese in the armed forces of Canada, these might be in danger of attack by "less responsible elements among their comrades".

But it was plain to the leaders of the Nisei that Japanese Canadians in uniform would be the most powerful factor in influencing public opinion for the good. A suggestion of an all-Nisei unit was turned down. One Nisei even rode the freights to Calgary hoping that anti-Japanese prejudice would not deter him from enlistment east of the Rockies, but to no avail. Pearl Harbour spelled finis to their struggle for enlistment, at least for a while.

But by 1943, the need for linguist personnel in the war against Japan was urgent, and only in Canada was there any large number of personnel who could be trained for the job. And as the focus of war moved closer to the Pacific, the need became more urgent. Thus the Intelligence arm of the Pacific Command urged enlistment of Japanese Canadians who could qualify for overseas service after a short course at S-20, the Japanese Language School in Vancouver. Forms were provided for Nisei in eastern cities; while in B.C., RCMP officers toured the ghost towns in search of men who would be interested in volunteering for special service--not with the Canadian Army, but with the British Army. Finally in February, 1945, a number of Nisei were to proceed to London for service with Lord Louis Mountbatten's South East Asia Command. But they were expected to cross the Atlantic in civilian capacity, and to enlist there in the British Army. The Canadian Army still would not accept them.

A sudden change in Canadian policy allowed this first group to be inducted into the Canadian Army. Without benefit of training, they embarked for India, on loan for special duties with the British Imperial Forces. The recruiting of Nisei volunteers began immediately after; by the time V-J Day came, Nisei were entering the service at recruiting depots across the country. About 150 were finally in uniform, almost all of them evacuees from the B.C. coast. Some of them aided the Allies in liaison work in the occupation of Japan, and others acted as interpreters and translators in India, Burma, Malaya and other far flung South East Asian areas.

III AFTER THE EVACUATION: THE ISSUES

1. Dispersal and Relocation

In his speech of August 4, 1944, Prime Minister King stated that it was desirable for the Japanese to be dispersed across Canada. Since this could be done by persuading the Japanese in B.C. to take work in the eastern provinces where there had been labour shortages, it was hoped that many of them would take advantage of the Commission's offer to pay rail fare, a small meal allowance, and a resettlement allowance to settle permanently.

Since the men who first went east in 1942 were successful in providing for themselves, the Department of Labour had begun to consider the possibilities of a larger-scale movement eastward. But the resettlement programme was never formulated as a policy until after the evacuation was completed. Rather, it emerged out of the relocation programme of temporary residence outside the "protected areas", which was all that had been thought possible when evacuation was carried out in 1942. Prior to 1946, however, resettlement did not mean the restoration of any of the pre-war rights of citizenship or the sense of freedom that the evacuee might have had. No resettled Japanese, for example, could acquire or hold land, grow crops in Canada, or buy houses. And some local councils, as in Toronto, refused to issue trade licenses. For those still in B.C., resettlement in the east imposed a difficult problem, especially since in the spring of 1945 all Japanese over 16 years were asked to declare themselves either as "repatriates" who would eventually go to Japan, or if unemployed in B.C. as resettlers willing to go "east of the Rockies".

Ontario and especially Toronto became the focal point of resettlement. At first about 700 were allowed to enter the city as residents and workers. But in the latter part of 1943 Toronto was made a closed city by the Board of Control. To many of the evacuees still in the evacuation camps, then, the east came to be known as an "unfriendly" area due to reports of the restrictions and spasmodic cases of race prejudice that occurred.

The decision to resettle in the east was one that assumed major proportions in the life of the evacuee still in B.C. It involved the taking of risks, breaking up the family unit in most cases, lack of training for new kinds of work, fear of the reported racial discrimination, and the general lethargy resulting from life in the ghost towns. Of the 15,610 Japanese in B.C. at the end of 1944, over 10,000 were living in ghost towns. And for these people, after the traumatic experience of the forced evacuation and the many painful experiences they had undergone, their confidence was low. And the future was uncertain and unclear. Moving once more would involve more insecurity and risks. The average evacuee disliked the crude discomfort and boredom of his interior B.C. abode, but feared and mistrusted the distant horizon more. A kind of dry rot had set in. In the early stages, it was only the more enterprising of the evacuees who did move eastward in an effort to establish themselves independently.

And although life in the interior settlements had many undesirable aspects, it did present a kind of haven from being bundled here and there by the government, and from rejection by Canadian society. Work, too, was available in interior B.C., and this was another temporary security that tended to hold the Japanese back from resettlement. In spite of efforts to get people moving in a second eastward evacuation, volunteers were few; the majority preferred to remain where they were. Thus by the summer of 1943 resettlement was going very slowly, and by 1944 it had almost ceased.

Efforts were made by the federal government to enforce resettlement. Extensive slashes in payroll in all interior towns were made so that no able-bodied men would be employed "except where absolutely necessary". Early in 1943, it was decided that unmarried Canadian citizens, males 18 to 55 years, who were unemployed would be subject to National Selective Service as would any other Canadian citizens. The evacuees reacted unfavourably to this because they had been evacuated on a basis of race rather than citizenship. And groups at New Denver, Kaslo, Lemon Creek, and Slocan sent protests and petitions to Ottawa. At the same time, because of the wartime labour shortage, various lumber concerns in the Kootenay area and orchard owners in the Okanagan Valley asked that evacuee workers be kept in the area until the end of the war.

But although the compulsory feature of the Selective Service was abandoned, and single males were once more allowed to take jobs in B.C., opposition was still raised against the newer plan of inducement; and often, people suspected of accepting eastern jobs were ostracized by others. Not until the segregation programme was put in effect in April, 1945, was there any great change in the increase of the number of resettlers. As a result of that programme, about two-thirds of the Japanese in Canada had moved outside B.C. by the end of 1946.

2. The Repatriation Issue

Probably the most important step taken by the government to settle for once and for all the problems of the restless evacuees was the segregation programme. Announced in 1944, it was started in March, 1945. In 1944, the anti-Japanese elements in B.C. had been unhappy with the lack of government pronouncements about the final disposition of the problem. The whole thing seemed to hang in the air. Several of the anti-Japanese MPs expressed their disappointment in the House of Commons, and they pressed for complete deportation of all Japanese, regardless of citizenship as the best and final solution.

On August 4, 1944, Prime Minister King stated that none of the Japanese in Canada, even the non-citizens, had been guilty of any offense against the security of Canada. But, he added, it would be desirable to try to determine the loyal and disloyal, and this latter group would be sent to Japan after the war. Mr. King's statement was an obvious compromise to the extreme demands voiced by the anti-Japanese agitators and the groups such as the CCF Party and the church bodies who wished to see justice and fair play prevail even in the emotional climate of wartime.

In B.C., the 1944 federal election campaign was organized partly around this issue. Led by John Bracken and Howard Green, the Progressive Conservatives demanded complete expulsion of the Japanese from the province whereas the CCF campaigned for rights of citizenship, and dispersal. Veteran Affairs Minister Ian Mackenzie headed the demand of the B.C. members of the Liberal Party for complete expulsion. He declared that he would forfeit his political life if the Japanese were allowed to remain in B.C.: "If the Japs are in, I'm out". Also, anti-Japanese groups such as the Richmond Japanese Repatriation League, made up of representatives of fishing and farming industries, took an active part in the campaign for repatriation. Another group, the Union of B.C. Municipalities, composed of representatives of every municipality in the province, resolved that every person of Japanese ancestry should be sent to Japan.

In early Spring of 1945, notices were posted in all interior settlements regarding "application for voluntary repatriation to Japan". Those who wished to remain in Canada were to re-establish themselves east of the Rockies as "best evidence of their intentions to co-operate with the government policy of dispersal. Failure to accept employment east of the Rockies was to be regarded as lack of co-operation with the government"... A short time later, members of the RCMP visited every interior centre. All persons over 16 were asked to appear individually before the officers and state their intention. These first steps were met with what amounted to jubilation by certain groups. Among these were the Federated Growers of B.C. and the Indian organization, the Native Brotherhood of B.C., who now felt that the Japanese could no longer threaten their new-found security in the farming and fishing industries.

Decision for most of the evacuees had little relation to any question of "loyalty" or "disloyalty" to Canada. Rather, it was based largely on personal circumstances and pyschological factors fermented by their wartime treatment. There was evidently a disbelief in the government and its policy, inspired and developed by experience since the evacuation. And there was the unhappy feeling that no matter where one may go in Canada, pronounced anti-Japanese feeling would manifest itself. Decisions of relatives and friends, family heads and family circumstances were determining factors in many cases. The majority of those who signed for repatriation signed because they were not prepared to accept the alternative of being forced to move east at the earliest possible date. They signed not because they wanted to go back to war-ravaged Japan but because even that seemed less repugnant than the prospect of trying to re-establish themselves in Canada in the face of existing restrictions, discriminations and hostility. Repatriation meant at least relief from unnecessary anxiety. In effect, then, the Japanese were given the alternatives of deportation to a land the majority of them had never seen, or settlement in a strange and hostile neighbourhood, on pain of being judged disloyal.

During the war, few Occidentals were concerned about the citizenship rights of the Japanese Canadians; indeed, as the Japanese attempted to resettle in the eastern provinces, there were few sustained protests against the restrictions that hampered them. The Japanese were largely left to themselves. After V-J Day, September 2, 1945, however, the tide turned, and protests were made in all parts of Canada against the repatriation programme which was still in process. The programme came to be defined as a threat to civil liberties and rights of citizenship.

Some 6,000 forms had been signed by those who signified their intention of going to Japan involving 10,347 persons, the majority of whom were Canadian citizens. In September, 1945, it was announced that plans were under way to transport the first of the 10,000 people to Japan. At that time the government introduced Bill 15 which contained a clause giving the government power over "entry into Canada, exclusion and deportation and revocation of nationality". The purpose of the Bill was to provide the government with transitional powers so that some of its wartime authority could be continued after the war had been declared as legally ended; that is, to provide the government with the legal basis for completion of its programme.

During October and November of 1945, the protest movement against this government action by the Japanese Canadian Committee for Democracy and Occidental groups gathered steam in the East. The rights of the Cabinet to issue an order-in-council for the cancellation of citizenship went too far for some Canadians who had awoken to the issues involved in the entire government policy. It was also put forth that the Japanese Canadian had a right to cancel his previous written declaration of intention of going to Japan. The government, after all, was seeking powers to revoke nationality and deport any citizen, loyal or disloyal, with or without consent, without right to appeal.

Of the total of 10,347 involved, 6,844 actually signed requests; the remainder were dependent children under 16 years of age. Those signing included 2,925 Japanese nationals, 1,451 naturalized Canadians, and 2,460 Canadian born. One-third of those facing deportation, therefore, were children born in Canada, and three-quarters of them were Canadian citizens. Prior to the surrender of Japan, some of them had sent in requests to Ottawa for cancellation, and after September 2, the requests had become more numerous. Minister of Labour, Humphrey Mitchell announced on November 21 that the government would not permit cancellation of requests by Japanese nationals, but would permit cancellation of requests of the naturalized if made prior to September 2, and review the Canadian-born cases. In short, if one had applied for cancellation before September 2, he was regarded as "loyal" to Canada; if he had signed after September 2, he was "disloyal". The government was therefore preparing to deport a large number of people against their wishes.

As a result of continuing and vociferous opposition from interested portions of the Canadian public, however, the offending clause was omitted. But this, in effect, meant nothing as Prime Minister King simply tabled orders-in-council to do what the clause had intended to do; that is, the government had the power to enforce deportation and to revoke nationality. In the debates of December 17, reaction in the House was bitter. Angus MacInnis (CCF Vancouver East) stated that the Japanese "were no more responsible for the military aggression of the Japanese Government than any other citizen of Canada", and despite "the way we treated them, despite the fact that we uprooted them from their homes; despite the fact that we denied them the rights enjoyed by every other citizen in the country, regardless of racial origin, not one disloyal act has been committed by any Canadian-born Japanese". He also pointed out that the treatment of the Japanese had "violated every democratic tradition and every Christian principle". MPs Thomas Reid and Howard Green, however, re-stated their anti-Japanese arguments, the latter even suggesting that the evacuees be re-settled in some area in the Pacific Ocean. Thus the future of the Japanese in Canada again became an acute political issue.

The three "repatriation" orders-in-council provided for the deportation of five different classes of people: Japanese nationals who signed requests for repatriation; naturalized persons who signed requests for repatriation and did not revoke them before September 2, 1945; Canadian-born citizens who did not revoke the request before the making of orders for deportation; wives and children under 16 of any to be deported; and Japanese nationals or naturalized persons recommended to be deported. Canadian nationality status was to be removed from these people.

Already in December, it was announced that the first 900 were to be sent to Japan on January, 1946. The Co-operative Committee on Japanese Canadians, which represented some 40 separate Occidental organizations concerned with safeguarding the rights of loyal persons of Japanese descent, directed its argument towards proving that the orders-in-council were "invalid, illegal, and beyond the powers of governor-in-council . It prepared for legal battle. The decision of the Supreme Court of Canada was not clear cut. A majority of the judges ruled that the orders-in-council were partially valid simply because the government had the power to do practically anything under the War Measures Act--and the government had rushed them through several months after the war was over, and only a few days before the Act expired. A majority also ruled it was illegal to deport the wives and children of the men being deported. Two of the judges further held that other parts of the scheme were invalid insofar as they applied to Canadian-born and naturalized citizens. This meant that the government could deport any person, but his wife and children would be left on the government's hands. And although the fight was carried to the last court of appeal, the Privy Council in London, this decision was sustained.

Yet, the sustained protest made the government decide upon an almost complete reversal of policy. On January 24, 1947, Prime Minister King announced that the orders-in-council providing for deportation had been repealed. Now, it meant that no one need go to Japan unless he wanted to, or if he was found guilty of disloyalty. Some 3,964 Japanese, however, voluntarily sailed to Japan; that is, only a little more than one-third of those who signed up actually went to Japan.

3. The Property Problem

One of the chief problems arising out of the enforced evacuation was that centering around the property of the evacuees. What was to happen to the boats, farms, machinery, tools, homes, furnishings, and personal possessions which they had to leave behind? That the government did not take adequate steps for the protection and preservation of property can be explained only in the light that the evacuation was a precipitate move, not one initiated on a broad plan nor as a permanent movement. The government provided no facilities for the protection of property while the evacuees remained in the "protected area", other than the formality of voluntary registration. The first instructions given the Custodian of Alien Property in March, 1942, were to assume management and control of property "as a protective measure only". That the removal had assumed permanent aspects came when the "protection only" was abandoned, and on June 29, 1942, with mass evacuation underway, powers of disposition by "sale, lease, or otherwise" of agricultural land was authorized, and again on January 19, 1943, such powers were extended to all Japanese properties. Thus all Japanese property, real or personal, was to be sold, although this property, stored with the Custodian, had been entrusted to him by the owners on the belief that he was to exercise protective control only.

Since the evacuees generally assumed that they would be permitted to return to their homes as soon as permitted, they resorted to makeshift arrangements for storing possessions. Some resorted to quick sales or to leaving their goods in community halls or churches. In many cases, only very brief notice to move was given, necessitating hasty action. Possessions could not be taken with them since restrictions were placed on baggage permitted for transport out of the "protected area".

Substantial losses were suffered. Theft and vandalism were common. The minimum amount of baggage, which the evacuees were allowed, consisted only of bare essentials for survival; the accumulated possessions of many years had to be left behind. Many articles were stolen from fishing boats while impounded; automobiles left at designated points were stripped of tools and even inner tubes and tires were replaced by those of poorer quality. Losses, then, included loss from income, loss due to sale price being lower than the appraised price, loss from items lost, stolen, or destroyed. Indeed, the list grew long.

First, fishing boats were disposed of without consent of the owners. Then the Director of Soldier Settlement took over 769 Japanese farms for the purpose of securing good, proved farm lands at a bargain price. This was done at a cost of about $893,390 in the face of assessment values totalling $1,250,000. Yasutaro Yamaga of Haney who had been appointed in April, 1943, to the Advisory Committee on Rural Japanese Property, resigned in protest over this action. And as he later inspected the farms in the lower Fraser Valley, it seemed to him that a million-dollar industry, the result of 35 years of slow work, was a thing of the past because of the neglect in the interim. Farm land sales did not proceed with a view to getting the owners a fair price. Sales of this type were unprecedented; there was no recourse to arbitration, nor any appeal to the courts as provided under the War Measures Act in case of expropriation by the Crown. Thus these sales gave opportunity for economic profiteering: it meant newly created business opportunities and unexpected possession of properties and chattels for many. Chattels such as radios and merchandise were auctioned, and under conditions of forced liquidation, the sales resulted in low-bidding and low prices. Boats and gear, real property, businesses and equipment, all suffered a similar fate.

Since the Japanese had gradually and painfully built up their material resources in the years before the evacuation, the liquidation of their assets proved to be a central problem. It was natural that they would protest. Numerous letters were sent to the

Custodian in Vancouver, and to departments of government in
Ottawa, but these were ineffective. In April, 1943, the Japanese
Property Owners Association started to organize, received
subscriptions from about 600 people in order to bring three suits
against the government, one each for a Japanese national, a
naturalized citizen, and a native born citizen. Most felt that they
had no chance of a fair hearing, but thought that at least one legal
test should be made. Petitions of Right were filed with the
Exchequer Court in October, 1943; and the case was scheduled to
be heard on May 29, 1944. But it was not until September, 1947,
that a decision was made public by Justice J. T. Thorson. He
simply announced that the cases were dismissed.

While waiting for this decision, the Japanese Canadian
Committee for Democracy after securing 200 claims from former
evacuees in the Toronto area, announced on January 24, 1947, that
evidence indicated about 75 per cent losses. Properties estimated
to be worth $1,400,395.66 had been sold for $351,334.86. Thus
losses incurred totalled $1,031,732.89. About this time, it was
evident that the government had no intention of investigating the
whole question of property claims; it refused to recognize that any
wide scale injustice had been done, and was prepared to make only
minor adjustments. But the newly formed National Japanese
Canadian Citizens Association and the Co-operative Committee on
Japanese Canadians pressed for more action. Finally, a claims
commission was set up by the government. Some 1,300 claims
amounting to over four million dollars were drawn up for the
government to review.

But it was not until the Spring of 1950 that Justice Henry
Bird of the Property Commission completed the hearings. The
Commissioner found that the amounts paid to the Japanese for their
land and chattels were substantially less than the fair market price.
He recommended payment of an additional $1,222,929. The greatest
undervaluation of real estate had occurred in the Fraser Valley
farm; and former owners received additional payments averaging
80 per cent of the original price. In other areas, the additional
payments did not rectify the losses incurred. The highest payment
was $69,950 to a central Vancouver Island Lumbering Corporation,
and the lowest was $2.50 for a motor vehicle claim. Although the
payments were considered "rough justice", they were, on the whole,
inadequate in view of all the factors involved.

IV RETURN AND RE-ESTABLISHMENT

As repatriation ships left Vancouver bound for Japan, and eastward resettlement gained momentum, the ghost towns in interior B.C. began to de-populate rapidly during 1946. Once again they resumed the deserted air they had four years before when the first evacuees stepped bewilderedly on the dusty streets. The Department of Labor set November 15, 1946, as the deadline for closure of the housing projects in the Slocan area and Lemon Creek. Other centres--Sandon, Greenwood, Kaslo, Tashme and Roseberry-- had already been closed. A sad chapter in the story of the Japanese Canadians was drawing to a finish as 1946 waned.

The end of the war did not mean that Japanese Canadians could return to the coastal area from whence they had come, nor did it mean that prejudice was disappearing. Indeed, officials of the Department of Labor, the office of the Custodian, and the RCMP expressed fear that a large movement of Japanese back to their former homeland might stir up the whole anti-Japanese feeling anew. The Vancouver Sun in December, 1946, said,

> "If they are to live in peace in Canada they must not revive any idea of re-establishment of a Pacific Coast colony . . . We must have ample assurances from the government that Powell Street and Steveston are to remain white".

And in February, 1947, the annual convention of the Army, Navy and Airforce Veterans of Canada urged extension of government controls over the movement of Canada's Japanese for ten more years. It said,

> "The return of this centrally-controlled dual citizenship foreign floc would operate as an insidious menace to all citizens in this area, particularly to our war veterans now seeking re-establishment in farming, fruit-growing, fishing and small business".

Prejudice was dying hard.

On the other hand, the situation led Professor H. F. Angus of U.B.C. to say that the government's exclusion of the Japanese from the coast was:

"an abuse of constitutional powers. The Japanese
have been accused of no crime by any responsible
authority, nor have they been wrong-doers like
deserters, or reluctant citizens like those who
evaded conscription . . . The defense zone is
in fact being used to force them to settle down
in other parts of Canada--an operation more
like the house-breaking of so many dogs".

But the time did not appear ripe for the return of the
Japanese. As Jack Scott, Vancouver Sun columnist, said in
January, 1947,

"Even today the writer who defends the rights of those
citizens of Japanese extraction can count on a flood
of vitriolic, hysterical mail".

Yet, in general, it appeared that the end of B.C.'s
Japanese "problem" was in sight. Left in B.C. were about 6,750
mostly scattered in the interior. There were about 700 persons,
mostly aged persons and invalid, at New Denver; and most of the
remainder had been continuously self-supporting since evacuation
in 1942. The mass exodus east of B.C. and repatriation had taken
the others. The great majority of those who moved east were
relatively well established and were spreading out into an unprecedented variety of jobs, businesses and professions.

In April, 1947, the B.C. Legislature passed a new
elections bill giving the vote to Canadians of Chinese and East
Indian descent, but still barred Japanese Canadians. Thus B.C.
still remained the only province where such a disqualification
remained in effect. Harold Winch, CCF leader of the opposition,
attacked the bill in his demand that all race discrimination in the
law be removed. "The bill shows", he said, "this government agrees
with the Fascist idea of making people second class citizens because
of their racial origin". The denial of the vote--an important
political disability--meant that discrimination in economic activities
would still be permitted and encouraged. But because the Japanese
in B.C. were no longer grouped as competitive economic blocs
inviting the attacks of Occidental competitors, the way to the
franchise seemed more hopeful.

Labor Minister Mitchell announced on April 23, 1947,
that restrictions on travel inside B.C. would still remain. Thus no
persons of Japanese descent could enter the coastal area, including
World War I and II Veterans, unless they had special permits from
the RCMP. All restrictions on movement of Japanese living east
of the Rockies, however, were lifted. Two Japanese Canadian
veterans, Buck Suzuki and Kingo Matsumoto, at this time were
refused licenses to fish in B.C. waters. The reason? The
Department of Fisheries stated that an emergency wartime order
restraining the issues of licenses was still in effect.

In its Christmas Issue of 1947, however, the New Canadian reported, "Situation Almost Normal--Six Years After Evacuation". Indeed, at that time, the compulsory deportation threat had been removed, and the evacuation property loss indemnification plan was an indication that the government intended to repay a part of the wartime losses. And a certain sense of security and achievement was created when delegates from B.C. to Quebec gathered at Toronto and organized the National Japanese Canadian Citizens Association to fight through organized effort for equal citizenship rights. The National body was to co-operate with its chapter in B.C. in the fight for enfranchisement and meeting employment problems in the province.

And there were lingering problems. Only a few weeks later, on January 27, 1948, it was announced that 800 Japanese loggers and sawmill workers of interior B.C. were to be placed in unemployment with the lapse of federal wartime regulations permitting the employment of Japanese on crown timber lands. Thus a 35-year-old law was to come back in effect; and a "war of attrition", as the Vancouver branch of the Canadian Civil Liberties Union phrased it, was still being continued, striking at the principal means of support of the Japanese still in B.C.

The B.C. Japanese Canadian Citizens Association immediately swung into action. All the local JCCA throughout B.C. were asked to contact the timber operators, lumber mill owners, union officials, Occidental organizations and individuals to gain support. The three representatives were sent to Vancouver to gain support in lower main land. Through support of three major newspapers and radio stations as well and all religious groups and Civil Liberties Union the public was informed of the situation. The result; a storm of protest forced the Provincial Government to suspend its order; revealing somewhat dramatically the change in public opinion toward the Japanese. Finally the representatives met with members of the Provincial Cabinet, obtaining from this body an assurance that British Columbia Timber Act employment disability would be temporarily suspended until the next legislature and also assures that this law including the mining law would be rescinded permanently and at the same time the enfranchisement of the Japanese Canadian was promised.

This suspension was an extraordinary achievement. Before the war the thought of allowing Japanese to work in Crown forests had been intolerable and politically impossible. Thus more progress in solving the problem of race and colour was being made during the last few years since the removal from the coast than in the previous half century.

Revocation of all special wartime restrictions still affecting Japanese in B.C. was urged in a brief submitted on March 8, 1948, to Prime Minister King and members of the cabinet by the National JCCA. But the government revealed four days later that federal restrictions which prohibited Japanese from moving freely into the Pacific Coast areas, or going into the fishing industry, would be continued until April 1, 1949. In April, 1948, two Nisei representatives were busy in Victoria in an attempt to secure action that would lift the ban on Japanese employment on crown timber lands, and to extend the vote to Japanese Canadians. They were George Tanaka, executive secretary of the National JCCA, and Hideo Onotera, president of the B.C. chapter. During his tour of Western Canada, Tanaka reported that the Japanese found themselves happier and better off economically in other provinces in Canada than they were in B.C. "Those who do return to B.C. probably will be very disappointed", he said. This seems to have been the general opinion.

In June, 1948, there was good news, for the House of Commons passed Bill 198 which enfranchised Canadian citizens of Japanese race living anywhere in Canada after March 31, 1949, without any outcries of protest from the B.C. members. But behind this somewhat easy winning of the federal franchise lay many years of heart-breaking toil and campaigning, stretching back 20 years or more. The removal of the franchise bar in the B.C. Elections Act loomed within reach.

The welfare and status of the Japanese in B.C. were improving steadily since the dark winter of 1945-6 when deportation had threatened. However, among the over 14,000 former evacuees now in the east, there seemed little likelihood that any great number would return even when restrictions were lifted. A new world of opportunity had opened to the Nisei in Eastern Canada, far different from the cramped life they had led in B.C. That the tide was swinging away from the fevered anti-Japanese agitation in the coastal area was exemplified when the Vancouver City Council moved to extend the vote to Orientals on January 17, 1949. The motion was passed by unanimous vote despite the fact that one-time foes of the Japanese such as the former Mayor J. D. Cornett and veteran Alderman H. D. Wilson were members of the council. The voices that were still being raised against the lifting of the coastal exclusion were those of people who feared direct competition from the Japanese. Said the Native Brotherhood (Indian) Organization in February, 1949, "We flatly do not want the Japs back in our coastal region". In the Fraser Valley, too, the Maple Ridge Board of Trade reflected the alarm of local farmers who feared the thought of Japanese coming back to the berry-growing industry.

Finally, on March 7, 1949, B.C.'s Japanese Canadians won the franchise as the legislature introduced an amendment to the Provincial Elections Act. This was without doubt one of the most important milestones in the Japanese Canadians' quest for equal citizenship rights. The stigmata of disenfranchisement was at an end. And with it, the "de facto" color bar which automatically shut them out of the more desirable occupations. A whole list of political and economic discriminations was washed away. It was a historic occasion.

Then seven years after the federal government in a series of orders-in-council imposed drastic restrictions on its West Coast Japanese, and almost four years after the end of the war, these restrictions were allowed to lapse on April 1, 1949. The Japanese could now return to the Coast. It was another day of sweetness and light. But it was a long time coming.

There was only a trickle of Japanese moving back to the Coast, however, and these were a few fishermen and gardeners returning from the interior. When the fishermen did settle back in Steveston and other fishing towns, relations with others in the industry were in general fairly good, though the Skeena Indians still protested vehemently. And the Japanese who now returned to Vancouver experienced only a few instances of discrimination. Most of them were employed in the City's sawmills during that year. But even one year after restrictions were lifted, April 1, 1950, only a few hundred of the original 22,000 had returned to the coast, and by another year, 1951, less than 2,000 had returned.

Thus there was no heavy back-to-the-coast movement by the evacuees. The idea of returning to the Coast appealed to only certain people: most strongly to those in interior B.C. and in Alberta than those who had moved farther east. But even among these people the actual number of persons who decided to return never reached a sizeable figure as to create a second Japanese "problem". At any rate, returning to the Coast was not like "going home".

The 1951 census returns showed 7,169 Japanese in B.C., representing one-third of the total Japanese in Canada. This was a startling change from the census ten years ago when the Japanese in B.C. comprised 95.3 per cent of the total in Canada. The 1941 total of 23,149 Japanese in Canada had also decreased ten years later to 21,663. And Vancouver, once home of the largest Japanese community with over 8,000 now only had 873. Thus the effects of the dispersal and resettlement had been widespread.

By 1958, about 8,300 Japanese were estimated to be living in the province. Vancouver's population, still the largest, had grown to 2,500, followed by Steveston's 1,200, and the Okanagan district's 1,000. And it is unlikely that these figures will change greatly since the situation, seventeen years after the evacuation, has definitely regained normalcy. It is also noteworthy that many of the former evacuees who were moved to interior B.C. have settled there permanently. Where there had been only a scattering of Japanese in interior B.C. before the evacuation, this region has become the permanent home for a considerable number. Slocan

City, Greenwood, Kamloops, Revelstoke, Nakusp, Lillooet, Kelowna, Vernon, and so on, now can count Japanese Canadians among their residents.

Today, a 1958 survey shows that the lumbering industry attracts the most workers among the Japanese in the province. This is followed by farming, industrial plant work, railroads, gardening, fishing, manual labour, government and clerical work, engineers, teaching and other professions, retail and wholesale businesses, small commercial enterprises. The public field is also open to them, not long after the lifting of restrictions, Dr. Masajiro Miyasaki of Lillooet was elected to a seat on the village council as commissioner. The Japanese are still rather proficient in strawberry growing: in 1952, Kaemon Shikaze of Dewdney was crowned as the Fraser Valley's "Strawberry King". And there have been other achievements since the return and re-establishment. The Vancouver Japanese Language School, first opened in 1905, was also reopened in September, 1952, with classes open to Occidentals. This time there was no attempt to re-introduce the old, almost compulsory, day school for primary students. And since there was a greater contact with the Orient, especially in relation to import-export business, leaders felt that a more general knowledge of the Japanese language would be beneficial. As an ironic comment on the changed times, one of the chief reasons for re-opening the school was to help enable Japanese Canadians to "bridge the gap between Japan and Canada".

CONCLUSION

Though the evacuation and its bitter aftermath now seem like a fading chapter in the history of the Japanese Canadians in B.C., to all of them old enough to remember it, it will always be a mental scar in their past. Ostensibly premised upon military necessity, it was committed without trial or any kind of hearing, and it remains as a blot on the province's history. True, the evacuation and the re-settlement brought new opportunities to most of the young people and largely dispelled the Japanese "problem" on the Coast, but the shock and economic loss to the older people cannot be measured. And it remains the most drastic invasion of civil rights which the war evoked, and the most drastic invasion of the rights of citizens of Canada by their own government that has thus far occurred in the history of Canada.

But for all its drastic character and its high cost in the impairment of human values, the evacuation was not without its benefits and compensations. In the years after the war, the Japanese Canadians in B.C. have regained their pre-war status and more, and have achieved a high degree of popular acceptance than had ever been accorded them since the first regular immigrants arrived at the province's coastal ports in the early 1880's. There is no doubt that it is the dispersal and resettlement, and the quiet and effective manner in which the Japanese Canadians have re-integrated and re-adjusted themselves into the wider Canadian community, and the hundreds of friends they have gained in the process, that have made for their easier acceptance.

Since the war, they have shown an increasing interest in activities and problems that they have in common with other racial groups and the broader community in the province. This is quite a different picture from the pre-war period when the bulk of them lived in self-contained settlements along the Coast. Now they are accepted, on the whole, as Canadians, sharing the rights and duties and a common destiny with others. It is with the lifting of restrictions, the decrease of extraordinary economic and political pressures that the Japanese Canadians have shown more interest in the development of normal social and economic interaction. And the elimination of the stigma of second class citizenship did much to bolster the self-confidence and well-being of the Japanese Canadians.

Today the life that was symbolized by Vancouver's Powell Street is now over. The concentration which was due to normal social impulse and to the entrenched antagonism of Canadian society itself is a thing of the past. The Powell Street of yore is the memory of another age, coming back in troubled moments or in snatches of sentiment.

Today in the present day Vancouver community, there is no real centre of geographic concentration, and unlike the pre-war period there is no closely integrated hierarchy of institutions and associations. And while it is generally thought that the economic level of the local Japanese Canadians compares favourably with that of their counterparts in the eastern provinces, the economic picture is much brighter. For instance, with the lifting of the enfranchisement bar, there are now lawyers and pharmacists among the ranks of the Japanese Canadian professionals.

Though probably in lesser degree than the former evacuees who had relocated eastwards, the Japanese Canadians in B.C. have also experienced the break-up of the rigid authoritarian family control that was exercised prior to the war. There is a far greater independence among the Nisei; it is they who now make the major decisions while the Issei, though they have recovered from the traumatic effects of the evacuation, remain in the background. Thus the second generation have definitely come of age; and to the growing Sansei (the third generation), the dark events of the past will only be a thing of wonderment to them.

And with the rising interest in the Orient and its culture among Occidentals, Nisei no longer need fear to eschew the exotic; rather, in a curious swing of time's pendulum, many of the Nisei now go out of their way to attain knowledge about the culture of Japan because they feel they can make a valuable contribution to the Canadian "melting-pot".

Finally, the Japanese Canadians have come to realize a new sense of the vastness and diversity of the province as well as the nation. No doubt they have become the most widely travelled group in Canada. Like other residents, and perhaps more, because it was brought home to them that they were unwanted, the Japanese Canadians have deeply felt the peculiar qualities that belong to British Columbia alone. They have tramped through the deep silence of the woods, looked across Burrard Inlet from Prospect Point at the city of lights on the North Shore, heard the fierce, proud silence of the mountains, felt the icy cold winters of the interior, tasted the sweetness of the Okanagan mackintoshes. In short, they have felt the spirit of place. The Japanese Canadians who remained in the province, or have returned to it, still feel it; it is within and without them.

To the others elsewhere in Canada who might visit their birthplace, returning to B.C. is a dispelling of a promise of a nostalgia-dripping sentimental journey. It is the hollow laughter of the ghosts of time; the umbilical cord of association has been

severed. Yet the vast amphi-theatre of Vancouver harbour sweeps
around the city with its unchallengeable mystery and allure of sea-
going ships, weaving around itself the chiaroscuro of romance.
And the Pacific whispers in the distance, a sound like in a shell, so
strange to a land-locked easterner. It is a beauty that flatters and
soothes the bruised spirit. It is the shape of lost years, the
unforgotten days, the hours of birth and destruction and re-birth.
Time is both a destroyer and a preserver.

** ** ** ** **

BIBLIOGRAPHY

This short history, written for the British Columbia Centennial Year, is a composite product based on the various sources that were available as well as the Writer's own experience. Although the Writer has gone over, in the course of research, most of the books, pamphlets, articles, newspapers, theses, etc., that were available on the subject, only the principal sources that proved most valuable are listed below:

E. Fowke, *They Made Democracy Work. The Story of the Co-operative Committee on Japanese Canadians.* Toronto, 1951.

F. E. LaViolette, *The Canadian Japanese and World War II.* University of Toronto Press, Toronto, 1948.

C. J. Woodsworth, *Canada and the Orient.* MacMillan Co. Ltd., Toronto, 1941.

C. H. Young, H. R. Y. Reid, and W. A. Carrothers, *The Japanese Canadians.* University of Toronto Press, Toronto, 1938.

Submission to the Royal Commission on Japanese Canadian Property, by the National Japanese Canadian Citizens Association. Toronto, 1948.

The files of *The New Canadian*, Vol 1, No. 1, November 24, 1938 to Vol. 21, No. 56, July 16, 1958.

Newspaper clippings from *Vancouver Daily Province*, *Vancouver Sun*, and *Vancouver News-Herald*.

CANADIAN JAPANESE

IN

SOUTHERN ALBERTA
1905 - 1945

by DAVID IWAASA

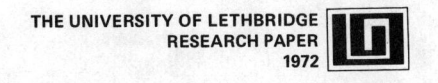

THE UNIVERSITY OF LETHBRIDGE
RESEARCH PAPER
1972

TABLE OF CONTENTS

PREFACE

INTRODUCTION

CHAPTER I   1905-1914   PAGE

   A.   The Arrival   1
   B.   The Railroad Workers and the Miners   7
   C.   Farming and the Sugar Beet Fields 10
   D.   The Cities and Towns   17
   E.   Japanese Society   19

CHAPTER II   1914-1929

   A.   World War I 26
   B.   The Good Years   29
   C.   The Raymond Buddhist Church 39

CHAPTER III   1929-1941

   A.   The Bad Years 45
   B.   The Manchurian Crisis and War in China   50
   C.   War with Germany   51
   D.   Pearl Harbour 54

CHAPTER IV   1941-1945

   A.   The 'Old-timers'   59
   B.   The Evacuees
      1.   The Sugar Beet Fields Again 63
      2.   Controversy 73
      3.   Acceptance   85

CHAPTER V

   The Foundation of A Future 93

APPENDIX

PREFACE

Forgetfulness is a rather common human trait. As a result, we are too often prone to forget the efforts and sacrifices of our predecessors. The large Japanese presence in British Columbia prior to the Second World War was often the subject of great controversy. Therefore, the relatively small numbers of Japanese in Alberta as compared to B.C. has meant that the Japanese in Alberta have enjoyed virtual anonymity as far as history writers are concerned. It would be extremely unusual to find even a passing reference in most history books to what at one time constituted the second largest concentration of Japanese in Canada.

Statistically, however, the Japanese in Alberta never formed a significant proportion of the population. Nonetheless, despite their small numbers they were able to make significant contributions to the economy and development of Southern Alberta. The early presence of Japanese in Southern Alberta also eased the way for many Japanese who were expelled from British Columbia in 1942 to remain and prosper. Another important point to keep in mind is that whereas in B.C. the Japanese were subject to many discriminatory statutes, no such regulations existed in Alberta. Japanese-Canadian residents in Alberta were allowed to vote, hold local and provincial offices, and to enlist in the armed forces. Therefore, the Alberta situation presents itself as an interesting comparison to the situation that existed in British Columbia.

This study, <u>A History of the Japanese in Southern Alberta: 1905 - 1945</u>, is only meant to be a beginning. Idealistically, I hope that this study will help to dispel misunderstanding and create a greater appreciation of the wonderful heritage of Southern Alberta. However, more realistically, I hope that this research will prompt others, more qualified and experienced than I, to conduct further studies.

I cannot claim complete impartiality, in that my grandfather was one of the early Japanese pioneers in Southern Alberta. The prime motivating force in this study has been my desire to learn more about my grandfather and in turn, more about my own heritage. Therefore, I dedicate this study to Mr. Kojun Iwaasa, my grandfather, to Mr. Toru Iwaasa, my father, and to the men like them who have played such a vital role in creating the future of Southern Alberta.*

---

*This study was made possible through a summer research scholarship from the University of Lethbridge, to which the author expresses his gratitude.

INTRODUCTION

A. Methodology

The research for this history was conducted along three major lines. First, extensive research was done into all previously published material. Second, representative individuals were interviewed and taped, concerning their personal experiences and material which they might have learned from other sources. Third, exhaustive cross-checking of information was done in which personal reminiscences were checked with published material, archival and newspaper accounts.

The first thing that was immediately encountered in the search for previously published material on the history of the Japanese in Southern Alberta was the almost total dearth of good material. What had been published was mostly recent material, and this was often unreliable because they were compiled from sometimes unreliable sources. However, two works by Junshiro Nakayama were found extremely invaluable, and they provided valuable clues as to what to look for in the interviews. Considerable work had been done on the Japanese in British Columbia, and this information assisted in learning more about the general Japanese situation. Often there would be a paragraph or two concerning the Japanese in Alberta, and this material again gave valuable clues concerning what to look for in archival and interview material. Most of the published material was found by searching through the bibliographies of the following works: The Canadian Japanese and World War II by Forrest E. La Violette, Canada and the Orient by Charles J. Woodsworth, and The Japanese Canadians by

Charles H. Young, Helen R. Y. Reid, and W. A. Carrothers. Many of the books were obtained through the inter-library loan facilities of the University of Lethbridge. The rest of the published material was discovered through visits to the Glenbow-Alberta Institute Library, the University of Calgary Library and the University of B.C. Library. A brief bibliography of material on the Japanese in Alberta is included in the Appendix.

The next step was to interview as many individuals as possible who might be able to remember details and experiences of the early period in Southern Alberta history. This work was extremely urgent because most of these individuals were very aged and often were on the verge of senility. Most of the very first Japanese in Southern Alberta are now dead, but fortunately a few still survive. These interviews concentrated mainly on the pre-World War II era, and emphasized reminiscences. Issei, or first generation Japanese, predominated because the emphasis was on recording the early history before these "pioneers" were unable to recount their experiences. An effort was made to interview those who were most representative. For example, a former coalminer who originated from Okinawa was interviewed concerning the early Okinawan coal settlements near Lethbridge. Two individuals, the daughter of an early Japanese restaurant owner and the wife of an early retailer were interviewed in Calgary to give information concerning the history of the Japanese in the Calgary region. The choice of who was interviewed depended upon how far away they lived, and whether they were available. Inevitably this led to a preponderance of Raymond and Lethbridge interviews. However, this can be justified in that the bulk of the pre-Second World War Japanese did live in the Raymond and Hardieville area. Also, many individuals from the outlying communities come to

Lethbridge in order to retire. Obviously, some people who should have been interviewed were not given the opportunity. The only excuse for these omissions is that time necessitated that some had to be missed. A list of all those interviewed along with the date of their arrival in Southern Alberta and the country and province of birth is included in the appendix.

Archival material consisted of newspapers, clippings, photographs, unpublished manuscripts and theses, and correspondence files. Particular mention should be made of the material available at the University of British Columbia Special Collections division and the East Asian Studies division. Also extremely useful was the material at the Glenbow-Alberta Institute Library. Some material was also obtained from the Alberta Provincial Archives, and the Legislature Library in Edmonton. Considerable material also came from the National Library in Ottawa through interlibrary loan. Many of the persons interviewed also had diaries and photographs. However, the time limitations allowed only very limited use of this material. Microfilm copies of the Lethbridge News and Lethbridge Herald were particularly invaluable, and the Lethbridge Public Library was very helpful in providing the microfilm and a reader. Before, any more original work can be done on the subject of the Japanese in Southern Alberta, more extensive research must be done in gathering and compiling archival material in the form of photographs and diaries.

B. Problems

A whole host of problems were encountered during the course of this research, not the least of them being the lack of previous work on the subject. Mr. Howard Palmer has completed a number of studies on the various ethnic groups in Southern Alberta, but unfortunately he has failed to go into enough detail on any one group in order to be of too much value in an in-depth study as this study attempted to be.[1] He did some very valuable work in doing a rather comprehensive newspaper study of the period from 1880 to 1920. Most of this work relating to the Japanese is published in an article entitled "Anti-Oriental Sentiment in Alberta 1880-1920", Canadian Ethnic Studies Vol. 2, No. 2, December 1970, Pages 30 - 58.

Nonetheless, despite the lack of material on the subject, what material that was available often conflicted. One example was the date of the arrival of the first beet workers in Raymond. Mr. Palmer in his book, Land of the Second Chance, the Raymond history called Raymond Roundup, and also a Calgary Albertan article all listed 1903 or 1904 as the date of the arrival of the first beet workers.[2] However, my own interviews with senior citizens of the era, both white and Japanese, led me to believe that 1907 or 1908 was a more accurate date. Subsequent searches through the Lethbridge News and also the Lethbridge Herald seem to confirm the spring of 1908 as the arrival date for the first Japanese sugar beet labourers. Another problem with previous works is that they often failed to list their sources of information. An attempt to remedy this situation was made in this research.

Newspapers also often did not give reliable information. Very often the early newspapers had a small staff and usually had to wait for the news to come to them rather than go out to seek the news. Therefore, the early reports were usually hearsay or the opinion of one or two persons. Dates and figures often conflict according to the report. However, the newspapers do give a very good indication concerning the situation and as long as one is not too fussy concerning specific dates and numbers, they serve as an excellent source of information. One often finds that people have a difficult time distinguishing between Chinese and Japanese. This means that often one is not sure whether a person is talking about Japanese or Chinese. Census figures are particularly misleading when they label individuals as 'Orientals' or 'Asiatics'. One interesting example of these problems is illustrated by the following article taken from the 1908 edition of the Lethbridge Daily Herald[3]:

WHITES BUY JAP CLOTHING

> Sam Ling of Thos. Kee and company tailors made the statement that were it not for the patronage of the white working men, his firm could not keep in business.

Obviously, the persons being referred to as 'Japs' in this article are Chinese. Other situations are usually not as distinguishable as this one but no doubt exist.

One of the most exasperating problems encountered in this study was one of language. In this area, the fault lies directly at the feet of the researcher. One of the best finds of this research were the books published by Junshiro Nakayama. His two books, <u>Canada no Hoko</u> and <u>Canada Doho Hatten Taikan</u> were both published in 1921 and they provide an extremely valuable commentary on early Japanese life in Canada and in Southern Alberta. However, these are both written in a somewhat literary style, and employ a great many Japanese characters that are not commonly used any more. As a result I was not able to utilize these books as much as I had wished. Often I had to have someone else read and explain passages to me and this would inevitably lead to some distortions and mistakes. Also this process was extremely time-consuming and in future studies, someone capable of reading and speaking Japanese fluently is required.

Time was another factor which dictated the manner in which the work was carried out. One summer is definitely insufficient a period for as vast a

subject as the history of the Japanese in Southern Alberta turned out to be.
A greater number of interviews should have been made. Much more work must
be done on the period just following the evacuation from the Pacific Coast.
Also a whole new story needs to be told concerning the Japanese in Southern
Alberta during the post-war period. These and other shortcomings become
obvious as one delves deeper into the study. Nonetheless, a little was
accomplished, and hopefully someone else will continue the study and
eliminate the short-comings.

  C. The Format of the Paper

  The format chosen for this paper is another item that is bound to
receive some criticism. In a study done by the Canadian Japanese Association
in 1940 entitled <u>The Japanese Contribution to Canada</u>, they list four
periods.[4] The first period is from 1885 to 1900 and is one of unrestricted
immigration. The second period runs from 1901 to 1907 and it is during this
period that the Japanese immigration reaches its highest peak. Also during
this period the greatest number of anti-Asiatic legislation is enacted.
The third period covers the two decades from 1908 to 1928. Period four is
the era from 1929 onwards. Obviously, this study uses immigration as the
key determinant in fixing the time periods.

  In this paper a more subjective criteria has been employed in dividing
the time period into five chapters. The first chapter deals with the
period from 1905-1914. Chapter two covers 1914-1929; chapter three covers
1929-1941; and chapter four covers 1941-1945. The last chapter discusses
some of the future trends and a few subsequent occurances.

  The reason why this study begins in 1905 rests on two items. First,
Alberta became a province in 1905, and prior to this period there was no

entity such as Alberta or Southern Alberta. Secondly, the first permanent settlement in Alberta, as far as we know, did not begin until after 1905. No doubt Japanese did work in Alberta or pass through the territory prior to this time, but we have no definite record of this other than what we could glean from the census records. The end date, 1914, was chosen because it was in this year that the Raymond Japanese Society was organized and also World War I began. These two events were important because they signified a change in Japanese status in Southern Alberta. The organization of the Japanese Society signified a changing of attitudes for some of the Japanese residents. No longer were they to be only transient laborers, but now they were attempting to better their lot in the community and also increase communication with the white population. The beginning of World War I signalled a change in attitudes by the white population to the Japanese around them. Since Japan was an ally, relations became better than ever before.

Chapter two ends in 1929 for two reasons. The most important one is the establishment of the Raymond Buddhist Church. For the next two decades the leaders and ministers of this small church were to play a crucial role in the culture and social fabric of the Japanese in all of Alberta, and 1929 was the year that the stock market crashed and markets throughout the world disappeared. The period 1914-1929 was one of relative prosperity for the Japanese. This is evidenced by the large numbers of wives that came to Canada during this period; their future husbands usually forwarded the fare to them. Relations within the communities were usually relatively good and so the depression and the Manchurian incidents heralded a new period of suspicion and discontent.

Pearl Harbour is the end point of Chapter three. December 7, 1941 was the end of a whole way of life for the some 23,224 Japanese in Canada at that time.[5] According to the 1941 Census there were 578 Japanese in Alberta as of June 2. By July 1, 1942, a little more than a year later there were approximately 3,160 Japanese in Alberta.[6] This was a 600% increase in a little more than a year! Chapter four attempts to chronicle some of the trauma and difficulties experienced by the 'evacuees' and also the local residents at that time.

1945 is a poor place to end, but an entirely new story begins with the end of World War II. Unfortunately, there was not sufficient time available to cover this period in this study. Hopefully, this subject will not remain neglected and other individuals will expend the time and effort necessary to do a comprehensive study of the post-war period in the history of the Japanese Canadians in Southern Alberta.

FOOTNOTES

1. Two major works by Howard Palmer are: Responses to Foreign Immigration: Nativism and Ethic Tolerance in Alberta 1880 - 1920. Edmonton, Univ. of Alberta M.A. Thesis, 1971 and Land of the Second Chance. Lethbridge, Lethbridge Herald, 1971.

2. Land of the Second Chance. op.cit., p. 112, J.O. Hicken (compiler). Raymond Roundup. Raymond, 1967, p. 40 and The Calgary Albertan. September 3, 1954.

3. Lethbridge Daily Herald. June 2, 1908.

4. Canadian Japanese Association. The Japanese Contribution to Canada. Vancouver, 1940, p.2.

5. Canada. Department of Labour. Report on Administration of Japanese in Canada 1942-1944. Ottawa, King's Printer, 1945, p.2.

6. Canada. Department of Labour. Report of Re-establishment of Japanese in Canada 1944-1946. Ottawa, King's Printer, 1947, p. 25.

CHAPTER I   1905-1914

A.   The Arrival

No one really knows just when the first Japanese arrived in Alberta. Perhaps they were some Japanese sailors shipwrecked off the coast of British Columbia who passed through the area now known as Alberta.[1]

> "In March, 1833, a Japanese junk, blown far off course was driven ashore near Cape Flattery. Its survivors were taken to Fort Vancouver and from there sent east across Canada by the Hudson's Bay Company to return to Japan by way of England."

Nonetheless, the first official record of the Japanese in Alberta and more particularly Southern Alberta comes from the Canadian Census figures. Although there appears to be some confusion as to the exact number of Japanese in Alberta the Census Records do indicate that some Japanese lived in Alberta prior to 1901. The fourth census of Canada conducted in 1901 lists 14 Japanese living in the North West Territories, which at that time included what is now Alberta. The sixth census of Canada lists 13 Japanese living in Alberta in 1901. It also states that 30 Chinese and Japanese were living in Lethbridge in 1901, although we may assume that the majority of these were probably Chinese. We have no record of exactly who these individuals were and what they did for a living, but they were most probably transient workers.[2]

The earliest Japanese, who came and stayed in Southern Alberta that we have a definite record of, is Kumataro Inamasu who arrived in Calgary on New Year's Day, 1906.[3] Mr. Inamasu came to Canada in 1900 and worked at the C.P.R. Hotel in Vancouver under C.D. Taprell. In 1905, when Mr. Taprell took over the Alberta Hotel in Calgary, he sent for 'Kemo', whom he thought highly of as a pastry cook. Mr. Inamasu spent Christmas Day on the train and started working at the Alberta Hotel on New Year's Day.

Mr. Inamasu arrived quite inconspicuously and with excellent recommendations, but such was not always to be the case. Southern Alberta was not immune to the prevailing prejudices. Often the local newspaper would print articles that were extremely anti-Oriental in nature. Usually these were just reprints from other publications, but occasionally local writers commented on the situation in British Columbia and in California, warning that similar problems would occur in Alberta.[4]

However, these local articles were conspicuous in their conservatism. An editorial in the Lethbridge News February 20, 1902 on the Anglo-Japanese Treaty which had created a violent controversy in British Columbia ended in this manner: "Nothing but the lapse of time and the fortuity of circumstances can prove the wisdom or otherwise of the treaty entered into by Britain and Japan." The editorial writer hints as to the possibilities of increased trade between Japan and Canada but no mention at all was made of immigration. This is extremely interesting in the light of later events because the Anglo-Japanese Treaty guaranteed the Japanese "full liberty to enter, travel, and reside in any part of the Dominion of Canada".[5]

A possible reason for this apparent lack of extreme anti-Oriental opinion could be the acute shortage of labour and population experienced throughout Alberta during this period. Ever since the Knight Sugar Company began operations in Raymond in 1903, they were plagued by a shortage of labour and this was one of the reasons cited for its eventual closure in 1914.[6] This was also probably the reason that prompted Premier Walter Scott of Saskatchewan to say in 1906 that Saskatchewan would welcome the Asiatics.[7]

The Calgary Herald argued in this manner:[8]

> "We have millions of acres of fertile land in Alberta which might lie untilled till Doomsday if we undertook to taboo on account of their colour, men, women, and children who are willing to come in and perform the hard and menial work."

Economics, therefore, was destined to play an important role in forming public opinion concerning the Japanese. As long as they were essential as a source of cheap labour, they were at least tolerated in Southern Alberta, albeit sometimes grudgingly.

This probably explains the dearth of comment concerning the following announcement that appeared in the Lethbridge Herald on August 21, 1906.

> "R.B. Nagatani of Kioto, Japan was in town last week on his way home from three years in the Guelph Agricultural College. He intends planting a colony of Japanese gardeners on irrigated lands in Alberta, and had come down from Calgary to look over lands here and at Raymond. He has decided to begin with two small colonies, one near Gleichen and one here."

The first Japanese came to Southern Alberta because they were needed -- in the sugar beet fields, on the railways, on the farms and in the mines -- and as a result, played an important role in the development of the area.

The Japanese in Southern Alberta came from a variety of areas. Most came to B.C. and then to Alberta, but there were some who came to Alberta via the United States. In 1907, Mr. Yoichi Hironaka was in Fernie working on the Great Northern spur line.[9] The majority who has resided in British Columbia for a short time were those who had either been frustrated in their efforts to accumulate wealth or were not satisfied with the restrictive situation that existed in that province and moved on to Alberta.[10] However, it would seem that the majority of those Japanese who came during the period from 1908 to 1914 either returned to B.C. or went to the United States. Communications between Southern Alberta and Utah and Idaho were facilitated by the large number of Mormons in the area. Thus, some of the very earliest contacts by Southern Albertans with Japanese were in Salt Lake City.[11]

The reasons for coming to Southern Alberta were varied. Mr. Yasaburo Yoshida gives three causes of Japanese emigration: increase in population, economic pressure, and inducement or attraction.[12] Population increase was definitely a factor because the population density per square ri (square ri equals 5.9552 square miles) in Japan grew in a little over ten years from 1,657 in 1892 to 1,885 in 1903. Concerning economic pressure, most of the individuals interviewed in Southern Alberta indicated that money was definitely a factor in their decision to come to Canada. However, one stated that he came to Canada to increase his knowledge, while another indicated that he was avoiding the draft. Most indicated that they had very little knowledge of the conditions that existed in Canada or in Southern Alberta, but they had heard that wages were high and that they could become wealthy. Often they simply equated Canada with the United States. Since 1907, it became more difficult for Japanese to emigrate to the U.S. mainland. Many came to Canada thinking that if they were refused entry into the U.S. that at least they would be on the American continent and someday would be able to emigrate to the U.S. However, one interesting discovery from interviews with the early Japanese residents in Southern Alberta is that many of them came from middle-class farmers. Some were even from relatively well-to-do families. None of those interviewed admitted coming to Canada to escape a desperate economic situation. This finding appears to be in harmony with the findings of Howard Sugimoto who makes this comment:[13]

> "Most of the Japanese immigrants destined for Canada came from the relatively well-to-do farming class, so that those who imputed that they were coolies showed a lack of familiarity with the Japanese social and economic structure. Few, if any,

coolies migrated to Canada for two main reasons. First, they
did not possess the money or the means to make the costly
arrangements and to pay for the voyage across the Pacific.
Second, they belonged to the very depressed class which did
not enjoy any of the cultural, social, or economic amenities
likely to have given rise to desires for emigrating."

The Japanese government was also very anxious to prevent anything from impairing its national prestige and so they were extremely strict in their screening of prospective emigrants. W. L. Mackenzie King in November of 1907 in a Royal Commission report commented that the Japanese government went to great lengths to "ensure within limits that no Japanese going abroad is likely to become a public charge on the country to which he has been allowed to emigrate".[14] Therefore it would seem that the prime motive of Japanese emigration was their desire to improve their position rather than the necessity of escaping misery at home.[15]

It was for this reason that inducement or attraction was an important factor in motivating Japanese immigration. The bulk of the some twenty interviews taken among early Japanese residents of Southern Alberta indicated that some other relative had travelled abroad before they had, either to the U.S., Hawaii, or B.C. This would tend to confirm that most of these individuals had come from families who had already demonstrated a desire to improve their lot and had an adventuring spirit. Compared to B.C. settlement, most Southern Alberta Japanese were late-comers and as a consequence most of them had been induced to come by relatives and friends who had already established themselves in British Columbia. Another important inducing factor was the labour contractors and the boardinghouse keepers. The Canadian Nippon Supply Company (Nikka Yotatsu Kabushiki Kaisha) was established on December 17, 1906, by Saori Gotoh and Frederick Yoshy. This company had an exclusive contract with the C.P.R. to supply Japanese labourers and their workers did considerable work in Southern Alberta. Other various independent contractors also played roles in bringing in Japanese labourers. The various boardinghouse keepers played a small but vital part by providing for the comforts of the Japanese as they arrived in Vancouver and referring them to various jobs.[16]

Another important cause of Japanese emigration was the general attitude of the country. Many individuals in Japan desired to learn more about the West and its institutions. Japan had just emerged from the semi-feudal Tokugawa era and was searching for new directions. The institutions and learning of the western nations were the symbols of greatness that they were attempting to assimilate. Travel abroad became exceedingly attractive to young Japanese students and many succumbed to the inducements of those who had gone before. School teachers also encouraged their young pupils to travel abroad and to study foreign languages. Once in Canada or the U.S. these young men tried very hard to keep up their studies, but usually gave up after a certain period and sought jobs as labourers. Therefore, among the Japanese labourers, often there were one or two extremely well-educated individuals.

Therefore, of the three causes of immigration: inducement played the most important role, with economics and population increase also as very crucial factors.

Judging by the statistics of Yasaburo Yoshida, who listed the number of passports issued during the five year period from 1899 to 1903, it would appear that there were emigrants from nearly every prefecture in Japan.[17] Rigenda Sumida, for his M.A. thesis, also noted that the Japanese in B.C. represented nearly every prefecture in Japan.[18] In 1918, Nakayama Unshiro compiled birth statistics in Raymond and he noted individuals from more than seventeen different prefectures.[19] In my own interviews I met with individuals from Yamaguchi, Fukuoka, Hiroshima, Nagano, Shiga, Ehime, Kagoshima, Mie, Okayama, Tottori, Tokyo, and Okinawa. Emigration was obviously not limited to people from one particular area. Although the Western half of Japan sent by far the most number of emigrants.

B. The Railroad Workers and the Miners

The turn of the century was one of extensive railroad building and the Japanese played an important part in this development in Southern Alberta. In 1903, Tadaichi Nagao who was working in British Columbia, received word to bring his labour crew to Medicine Hat.[20] They were employed in the shops at Dunsmore and on the line between Lethbridge and Swift Current, Saskatchewan. In 1906, the Canadian Nippon Supply Company took over the supplying of labour to the C.P.R. This company supplied not only the labour but also the supervisors and foremen under whose direction the men were to work. The contracting company simply made a single payment to the Canadian Nippon Supply Company. The the individual labourers were paid by the Supply Company in accordance to the agreement arrived at between the individual and the company. The men were charged one dollar a month by the company for its services, and they also furnished on commission supplies of food, clothing, and sometimes tools as well. A fee of fifty cents a month was charged to meet hospital expenses and another fifty cents for handling mail.[21] On August 10, 1907, the Canadian Nippon Supply Company cabled Mr. J.S. Milne, C.P.R. superintendent at Medicine Hat, that thirty labourers were on their way to Medicine Hat.[22] Then in 1908 some 600 labourers came into the Southern Alberta area.[23] In April of 1908 the *Lethbridge Herald* made the following quote: "200 Japs are to be employed on the construction work of the Macleod-Lethbridge cut-off so the Macleod Chronicle says."[24]

During this period, we see the first signs of opposition from organized labour in Southern Alberta. In the May 23, 1908 edition of the Lethbridge Daily Herald, the Herald labour editor quotes the following letter from the Taber correspondent:

> "Sir: Are the C.P.R. to be congratulated for their great philanthropy in importing over 70 Japs for the repairing of their line here? We drew attention on Monday last to the importation to Raymond of about the same number. Surely there are more than sufficient of the white race in the country anxious and willing and not able to get it."

This becomes the typical labour complaint.

The C.P.R. mechanics strike August 1908 was very crucial to the Japanese. In Medicine Hat the Canadian Nippon Supply Company provided over 300 workers, under Tokio Mukaide.[25] At Lethbridge the following headline appeared in the Lethbridge Daily Herald: "Four Japs at Work in the Local Shops".[26] On July 31, four Japanese arrived and the Herald emphasized that they were only working in the shops cleaning up the engines and changing the water. On August 1, eight or ten more Japanese arrived, but they were working in the yard, doing labourers' work only. Apppoximately 300 Japanese mechanics were distributed throughout the divisional points in the west. Mr. Taro Kanashiro, who was in Lethbridge during this strike, said that there was considerable feeling against the Japanese at this point.

However, we begin to see organized labour dividing into two groups having opposing attitudes concerning the Japanese. The first agitated for the expulsion of all Asiatics from Canada. In 1908, the twelfth item in the platform of the Independent Labour Party of Lethbridge was the exclusion of Asiatics. This party was formed by labour elements in Lethbridge, to contest in the Lethbridge Provincial constituency.[27] In 1907, the Coleman iner was quite adamently against union membership for Orientals.[28]

"You will have to sleep in the same boarding houses with them, eat at the same tables, wash in the same wash houses with them, and catch their foreign diseases. They will be your companions...Even worse, the "captains of industry" could cross-shift a 'miserable Chink of Jap" with a union man in order to get rid of him".

The other group began to agitate to unionize the Japanese, thereby ullifying their usefulness to the capitalists. This was illustrated by he announcement by R.R. Pettipiece in Winnipeg, who intended to run as socialist member from the Medicine Hat Federal Constituency, that he anted to organize a Japanese union in B.C.[29] Frank Sherman, a leading labour eader, introduced a resolution in 1909 in which Orientals were allowed to nter the union in District 18 of the United Mine Workers of America which ncluded all of Alberta.[30]

In British Columbia, the Japanese began working in the coal mines very arly in the century. However, it wasn't until 1909 that that first Japanese ame to Hardieville to work in the Galt coal mines. He was Jiro Ide, from kinawa.[31] At first he encountered considerable opposition and racial iscrimination, but his hard work and knowledge of karate eventually won the eluctant admiration of his work mates. In time more miners were attracted o the area, most of whom were from Okinawa. The work was extremely hard ut the pay was attracted them to the area, most of whom were from Okinawa. The ork was extremely hard but the pay was attractive at from $2.40 to $2.85 er day. The majority of those who eventually worked in the mines had come nto Southern Alberta with the Canadian Nippon Supply Company and had riginally been working on the railway gangs. Attracted by the higher pay, hich at times was as much as a dollar a day more, these men quit and came o the mines.[32] The normal procedure was for one or two to join the company and then to get their friends onto the payroll with the original member acting as an informal boss. Later, they were recognized as foremen and eventually even directed white crews. Most of these men were single and were only interested in making quick returns. It wasn't until the 1920's that many families settled in the mining towns. Japanese began working in Hardieville, Coalhurst, Diamond City, Staffordville, and Lethbridge.

Acceptance in the railroads and in the mines came slow. However, as time progressed and the Japanese became more integrated into the communities they began to be accepted as co-workers. The existence of a great number of other nationalities such as Italians and various Eastern Europeans created a very cosmopolitan atmosphere and most likely facilitated acceptance and integration.

C. Farming and the Sugar Beet Fields

The area in which perhaps the Japanese have had the most prominent influence is in agriculture. Japanese-Canadians pioneered the vegetable crop industry in Southern Alberta, and supplied a valuable proportion of needed labour in many of the other agricultural crops in the area. However, it was not easy for the first Japanese farmers. They had to overcome many hardships and disappointments in order to succeed. Southern Alberta was an alien environment for these men, most of whom were young and still single, and it required courage and fortitude to withstand the many difficulties that confronted them.

The first farming venture in Southern Alberta was centered near a small community just east of Calgary. In 1905, a Mr. Takeimon Nagatani came through Calgary and read a local newspaper article which lauded the virtues of farming in Alberta.[33] Having been educated in Canada at the Guelph Agricultural School, he was much attracted to the area and later returned to take out a lease on some 10,000 acres of farmland. He also visited Raymond in 1906 and was very interested in the sugar beet industry situated there. He even expressed an interest in setting up a colony of Japanese in the Lethbridge area.[34] Mr. Nagatani then returned to Japan and attempted to arouse interest among other potential Japanese promoters. He put out advertisements stating that he was looking for people who were seeking adventure and willing to go across the sea to find success. Mr. Nagatani was obviously a very ambitious individual and he went about selling shares in his venture. However, various problems occurred and only 13 men came with him from Japan in 1906. Once in Alberta, problems began to multiply one upon the other. The men were unaccustomed to the extremes in temperature in Alberta and were unfamiliar with prairie farming methods. As Nagatani's grandiose plans failed to materialize the men began to dessert either to Calgary or to other farms in the area. There was a reorganization of the financing of the project, and in 1907, the Canada Kono Kaishu imported more men from Japan. An individual by the name of Konosuke Otsuki became the organizational leader. Then in 1910, a Mr. Eiichi Kawakami became the leader, followed by a Mr. Iwanaga. Mr. Kawakami brought out his wife and attempted to put the colony on a more secure footing, but hail and inexperience doomed the experiment as a failure. For a while Nagatani opened an office as an engineer, but he eventually gave up himself and moved to Raymond where he ended up working with a Chinese market gardener.[35] Although Nagatani's original plans had failed, a few of the men he had brought out remained in the area, and later became successful farmers.

Mr. Nagatani's project at Cheadle and another project initiated by the C.P.R. created considerable controversy. In 1907, the C.P.R. contracted with the Canadian Nippon Supply Company to import 1000 Japanese labourers to construct an irrigation system near Gleichan, Alberta.[36] Considerable opposition was voiced concerning these projects, and several complaints were voiced in the Dominion House of Commons. 1908 was a federal election year, and an attempt was made to make the entry of Japanese into Alberta a political issue.[37] As a consequence, the Lethbridge Daily Herald announced in April of 1908 that Sir Wilfred Laurier had set up a special committee consisting of Mr. Carvel, Mr. MacDonald and Mr. Geoffrion - Liberals; and Mr. Barker and Mr. Lennox - Conservatives, to look into Japanese immigration into Alberta.[38] In another issue of that same paper, the following election advertisement appeared:[39]

                                       Liberals Refuse to Agree to Entry
                                            Cranbrook, Oct. 4, 1908

Hon. Frank Oliver
Edmonton, Alberta
        Conservative Candidate Goodeve asserts Laurier Government has established Japanese colony in Northwest. Also has set aside there 28 townships for Japanese. Is this so? Wire answer to Moyie, B.C.
                                                    Smith Curtis

Moose Jaw, Oct. 6, 1908
Smith Curtis
Moyie, B.C.
        Yours of Oct. 4th. Report C.P.R. has sold some irrigation lands east of Calgary to Japanese. Dominion Government refuse to agree to entry of Japanese colonists as being contrary to agreement with Japan. Statement in telegram utterly untrue.

                                                    Frank Oliver

Also in the House of Commons, Mike Herron announced that, "I never did and never will favor any class of people coming into our country and settling in bulk as a colony...Japanese will close up our other sugar factories and drive out the whites."[40] Out of the 1000 originally planned, only some 370 ever actually arrived in Alberta, and the majority of them did not remain for very long.

The largest and most permanent of all of the early Japanese settlement attempts occurred in Raymond. Prior to the coming of the Japanese, the Knight Sugar Company had been perennially plagued by labour shortages. In 1904, they attempted to use Chinese labourers and they brought 50 in from the coast, but they did not prove to be a success; and they gradually drifted off into other more profitable enterprizes.[42] However, even in 1906 mention was made of some Chinese working along with native Indian labour.[43] Considerable effort was made to obtain a provincial subsidy and they did receive some assistance in 1907. Great pains were taken to emphasize that beet sugar made in Raymond was practically the only sugar sold in Alberta that was not produced mainly by coolie labour.[44]

> "Those who object to the employment of coolies instead of white labour should insist on getting sugar produced by white labour; that is, beet sugar."

However, in 1908 the following quote from the Raymond Rustler appeared in the Lethbridge Daily Herald; under the headline "Jap Leases Beet Lands".

> "Fifty men from the Flowery Kingdom will raise beets at Raymond. The Rustler says: We had a very pleasant talk with Mr. Naykayama (sic) a wide-awake, aggressive, enterprising businessman. He impresses one at once with his preciseness, foresight and vigor. Moreover, he is as polite and courteous as the proverbial Frenchman, and meets you with a nod and pleasant smile. Understanding the English perfectly and talking it with a grace and freedom that would shame some born in the 'mother tongue', his conversation was both interesting and entertaining. He said that he had met Mr. Ellison in Salt Lake City on January 10, 1908 and had ther contracted with him for the lease of the beet sugar lands of the company comprising a little over 900 acres in the near vicinity of the factory. He said that within the next month he expected to have about 50 Japs here who would be brought in from B.C. Naykayama has spent considerable time in Utah and the inter-mountain region. He has been engaged in contracting

railway and farm work for the last fifteen years and is well acquainted with the requirements of the company in the particular regard. For some time he operated a gang in ogden. The presence of these Japs will answer one of the biggest problems that has confronted the factory since the inception and it seems absolutely impossible at present to get along without them."

Again various problems ensued and because some of the men brought in for the work were either unsuitable or unable to accustom themselves to the climate. In all some 100 workers came as a result of Mr. Bueimon Nakayama's efforts.[46] They were housed in small converted granaries and did most of the thinning and harvesting for that year. The crop was good that year but the workers made only fifteen or sixteen dollars after a years work.[47] That fall the majority of the original workers left and returned to B.C. Although some difficulties were experienced and Mr. Nakayama left after some disagreements with the management of the sugar company, this first attempt to use Japanese labourers in the sugar beets proved quite successful. The following quote came from the Calgary Albertan:[48]

"the Raymond company this year has better results from the beet raising on account of the considerable number of Japs who have come in and who have made good in raising the beets."

The first winter these men experienced in Raymond was very severe. Mr. Sudo remembers reflecting several times during that winter upon why he had ever come to Alberta.

In the Spring of 1909, Mr. Ichiro Hayakawa brought in some 105 men to break land for the Knight Sugar Company. They contracted some 1700 acres and everything went quite well.[49] In 1909, Kojun Iwaasa, Enzo Tachikawa, and Takashi Karaki arrived in Raymond. In 1910, through the encouragement of Tomosaku Otake, Zenkitchi Shimbashi arrived in Raymond. They worked in the various camps organized by the Knight Sugar Company in and around Raymond. Other nationalities also had their camps, and during this period a great many Belgian workers were also brought into Raymond area.

All of this activity by the Japanese in the Raymond area did not go unnoticed by people in the district. In June of 1908, the labour editor of the Lethbridge Daily Herald made the following comment:[50]

> "While the Japs and Chinks have up till recently been knocking at the door of Alberta. I regret to see that they have now crossed the threshold and located at Raymond where a big bunch of them are to grow sugar beets, and this, mark you, for the benefit of an industry that receives a bonus from our Provincial House."

The location of the Japanese in Raymond also became somewhat of a political issue. In July of 1908, Mr. C.A. Magrath, prominent local entrepreneur, addressed the members of the Lethbridge labour unions as the Conservative Party candidate for the Medicine Hat Federal riding. The Herald reporter gave the following account of what happened at that meeting:[51]

> "It appears to concern some people that there were some Japanese working at Raymond. He (Mr. Magrath) admitted being interested in the Raymond Sugar Company but his influence in it was not considerable. But he would not hide behind the company. The fact is that they are employing Japs because they could not get anyone else. No fair minded man could deny them the right to get the labour wherever they could.
> T.S. Harold wanted to know if Mr. Magrath would endorse the employment of the Japanese in Raymond. He could give the Raymond people all the labour they wanted.
> In reply Mr. Magrath said that the labour was wanted in certain seasons. They had to chase after Indians and others or lose their crops as they had done during the last year. If Mr. Harold could supply the labour when wanted they would not get Japs to do it.
> D. Quigley asked concerning the bounty asked for by the sugar company giving as their reason that they had to compete against Oriental labour.
> He did not endorse the employment of Orientals, he was opposed to it, but what could be done.
> Another gentleman asked if this was his own view or that of the Conservative Party. Mr. Magrath stated that it was his own view. He had not discussed it with Mr. Borden."

Mr. Magrath's viewpoint is very interesting considering the rather openly anti-Oriental views of Mr. Robert Borden, leader of the Conservative Party.[52] This again proves that economic necessity and the extreme shortage of labour caused many individuals to temper their views concerning anti-Asiatic agitation. In the October 26, 1908 election Mr. C.A. Magrath won the Medicine Hat Riding, although the Liberals under Laurier won the election. The interesting point to notice in this election is that although normally Conservative, Raymond voted for Mr. W.C. Simmons, Liberal candidate.[53] Mr. Magrath's moderate views concerning Japanese immigration obviously did not help him in the area where a large number of Japanese were working.

As the Japanese became more settled in Raymond, they began to purchase farmland of their own. Many of them received valuable experience working on the Knight Sugar Factory farm, giving the men a better background for independent farming. Some of the early Japanese pioneers mentioned that before working in Southern Alberta they had never even ridden a horse before. From the Mormon farmers in the Raymond area, the Japanese gained practical experience in the methods of irrigated farming which was to prove extremely valuable. The initial working experience in the Knight Sugar Company farms and ranches proved to be a very opportune one for the Japanese because it provided an excellent preparation and training ground for them to learn how to farm in Southern Alberta.

Prior to the First World War, several Japanese began to farm independently, either as co-operatives or individually. Yoshio Hatanaka, Seichi Tobo, Uemon Sakuma, Mr. Okuma and Mr. Iwakiri bought 40 acres and rented an additional 80 acres. Mr. Taseburo Takeda, Sakutaro Saga, and a Mr. Yamamoto purchased 160 acres, while Mr. Takejiro Koyata, Tanesaburo Kosaka, Kisaburo Sugimoto, Shoichi Tobo, and Hidematsu Isoda purchased another quarter-section together. Mr. Kojun Iwaasa purchased a quarter-section on his own, and in time some of the other groups broke up and they also began to farm individually.

In 1910, some Japanese began to raise potatoes and other vegetables for sale. Among the earlier ones were Mr. Tomosaku Otake and Mr. Hikokuma (Paul) Nakamura. A series of droughts and crop failures caused many of the early farmers to quit and return either to B.C. or to Japan and in 1910, only some 60 men were still working in the area. It was also during this period that Ichiro Hayakawa left for Calgary and a portion of his large lease was taken over by Mr. Tasaburo Takeda. Mr. Takeda returned to Japan and advertised for more workers, but only succeeded in convincing Mr. Eiji Tamaki to return with him and invest some money in the venture. However, in 1911, there finally was a good crop and the future began to look a little brighter. In 1913, the Japanese organized a small vegetable co-operative and sent some ten carloads of vegetables, mostly potatoes, directly to Calgary.[54] In a sense this was the modest start of the present multi-million dollar vegetable and potato industry of Southern Alberta.

By the time of the outbreak of the First Great War, the Japanese in the Raymond area were beginning to set down permanent foundations and were starting to play a modest role in the agricultural development of Southern Alberta.

D. The Cities and Towns

During this very early period not very many Japanese chose to live within the three cities and numerous small towns of Southern Alberta. Somewhat different than the Chinese, the Japanese did not immediately drift to the towns to begin small grocery stores and launderies. In Calgary, however, a considerable number of bell-boys red-caps were working in the various hotels, most particularly in the Alberta Hotel. In 1908, a Mr. Kinji Ohama owned a laundry and pool hall in Calgary and, in 1911, operated a

small market and rented ten acres of land in conjunction with one other
person. Similarly, Yaichi Iguchi also opened a market in Calgary. The
former Raymond resident, Ichiro Hayakawa, opened two western restaurants in
Calgary and prospered. Three Okinawans -- Makishi, Ano, and Oshiro opened
a pool hall in Calgary also. The 1909 edition of a booklet called <u>Canada
Doho Hatten Shi</u> (Development of the Japanese in Canada) published by the
Tairiku Nippo Newspaper lists four people in Calgary: Kanehitchi Matsumoto;
Kaizo Kamaji, who operated a fruit shop; Inamasu, a labourer; and Yasuzo
Murata, who was with the Canadian Nippon Supply Company.[55] In 1913, a Mr
Soemon Sugizaki opened a silk importing shop but unfortunately this did not
do very well and closed again in 1915. Banff also had some Japanese working
in the Banff Springs Hotel and the Hotel Lake Louise as bell-boys, and
kitchen staff. A Mr. Taniuchia also had a small shop there.[56]

In Medicine Hat, a Mr. T. Fujizaki worked in the Royal Hotel in 1909.[57]
The <u>Canada Doho Hatten Shi</u> mentions only one in Medicine Hat, a Mr. Ritsu Ide,
who worked for the Canadian Nippon Supply Company. It also lists two
residents in Lethbridge: Mr. Seinoske Bozako and Mr. Chujiro Higuchi, both
listed as miners.[58] Mr. Yoichi Hironaka was also another early resident of
both Lethbridge and Raymond. In Lethbridge, he worked as a cook at the
Dallas Hotel, and a short while later came to Raymond and opened a restaurant.[59]
Zenkitchi Shimbashi took Mr. Hironaka's place in the Dallas Hotel in 1912 as
a dishwasher and later as the second cook. But the management of the Hotel
changed, and about 1914, he worked as a cook at the Lethbridge Gaol. Then in
1915, he came to Raymond to take over Mr. Hironaka's restaurant.[60]

Generally speaking, the Japanese did not congregate in the cities of
Alberta, and no 'Little Tokyo' was created in any of the cities of Calgary,
Lethbridge or Medicine Hat.

E. Japanese Society

Life was simple for the early Japanese settlers in Southern Alberta. It consisted mainly of two things -- work and sleep. Before leaving Japan most of them were told "kokyo ni nishiki wo kazatte kaerinasai" (return home in glory, or come back rich and successful) and so they generally expected to work really hard for three or four years, and then return home to Japan rich. However, it didn't take long for most of them to realize that success and riches were not to be had quickly. Many of these early pioneers could not adapt themselves to the severe climate and strong winds and left after one or two years in Southern Alberta. Still others died and remain buried in unmarked graves along the railroad tracks. One young man died in Raymond during the winter of 1910, and his gravestone is still discernable in the Raymond cemetary, written curiously enough in English. For those that decided to remain in Southern Alberta, life was extremely difficult. In Raymond, the large number of Japanese allowed them to cooperate and assist each other. During these hard times, Kojun Iwaasa assisted in forming a small credit union among the Japanese which loaned out money and credit to provide scarce working capital.[61] Other Japanese also joined together for social and economic reasons. In February 28, 1909, the first chapter of the Japanese Association "Nihonjin Kai" was organized in Calgary with Konosuke Otsuki as chairman and nine others. However, membership was small and very little activity was carried out because of the fluid nature of the membership.

The Japanese during this period did not associate widely with the white population of Southern Alberta. Since most of the men did not speak English very fluently, there was not a great deal of contact between the two groups.

However, the presence of a large number of other ethnic groups in Southern Alberta meant that the early Japanese were at least tolerated and, other than in the railroad and mining fields, very little racial prejudice was evident on the surface. Those Japanese that could speak some English; such as Nikokuma (Paul) Nakamura, Yoichi (Harry) Hironaka, and Kojun (Henry) Iwaasa played an important role as interpreters in a variety of situations. They were called upon to negotiate land contracts, help purchase machinery, settle differences between the local residents and the Japanese and even to appear in court on behalf of Japanese residents.[63]

It is also interesting to note that many of the common Japanese prejudices were also prevalent during this period. Most of the early Japanese tended to create acquaintances from among their own prefectures and social classes. Very little contact between Okinawan people and other Japanese existed during the early settlement era. The common excuse was that many of the Okinawan people did not speak Japanese fluently and therefore, there was little reason to associate with each other. Nonetheless, as their length of stay in Canada increased, they began to shed more and more of these previous prejudices.

Since the majority of the first Japanese in Alberta were single, various moral problems were bound to appear. Almost all of these men were in their 20's, and those in railroad work or in the mines were in possession of ready cash. As a consequence, various individuals were quick to capitalize on this market. In 1909, there was a Japanese prostitute in a little town outside of Medicine Hat. Ironically enough the proprietor would not allow her to entertain any Japanese visitors, fearing that she might run away with them.[64] Others could be found in the various mining towns surrounding Lethbridge. These were not usually full-time women of pleasure, but rather

plied their trade while working in boarding houses and gambling houses. Often
they were simply the wives of the proprietors. Gambling also flourished in
the railroad camps and among the early miners and farm labourers. However,
one could hardly describe these activities as examples of the low moral character of the Japanese settlers. Rather these were simply isolated incidents
of individuals willing to satisfy the natural desires of a large number of
young unmarried men deprived of any social activities.

Many of the more responsible Japanese in Southern Alberta were also
aware of the moral problems of the young men and attempted to do something
about them. In 1914, the Japanese residents of Raymond organized the Raymond
Nihonjin Kyokai, (Raymond Japanese Society) and also the Meiro Seinenkai
(youth group). This was a locally inspired movement by the Japanese to solve
their own problems through cooperation. The Nihonjin Kyokai had five main
objectives: 1. to promote the social well-being of the Japanese in Raymond;
2. to create better relations and greater cooperation with the white residents;
3. to stimulate the progress and development of the Japanese in Raymond;
4. to provide financial assistance to those Japanese in need; and 5. to
assist in bringing more Japanese farm labourers to Southern Alberta.[65] The
first president was Mr. Kojun Iwaasa, who was followed by Tasaburo Takeda and
Yoshio Hatanaka.

The organization of the Raymond Nihonjin Kyokai was a milestone in
Southern Alberta Japanese history because it signified two things. First,
that the Japanese in Southern Alberta, and more particularly Raymond, were
attempting to solve some long-range problems among their own members. Secondly,
the Japanese were now signifying their readiness to integrate and cooperate
more fully with the other members of the community. Both of these points
indicate that the Japanese had decided that their future now lay in the land

of their adoption -- Southern Alberta.

FOOTNOTES

1. Dr. Stanford Lyman. "The Japanese Immigration to North America", The Oriental in North America. Lecture No. 7, Feb. 21, 1962, p. 4.

2. A man named Makishi is said to have arrived in Calgary in 1901, mentioned in Howard Palmer. Land of the Second Chance. op.cit., p. 112 (no source given).

3. Interview with Miss Mary Inamasu, and an article "Calgary Issei Well Known on Continent for Horses", New Canadian. Aug. 1952(?).

4. Editorial. "The Japanese Question", The Lethbridge Herald. Oct. 3, 1907.

5. C.J. Woodsworth. Canada and the Orient. Toronto, Macmillan Co. of Canada Ltd., 1941, p. 293.

6. Southern Alberta News. Dec. 14, 1906.

7. Lethbridge News. Aug. 8, 1906.

8. Calgary Herald. Feb. 1, 1908.

9. Interview with Dr. Robert Hironaka.

10. In Sept. 1907 extensive racial rioting occured in Vancouver.

11. Junshiro Nakayama. Canada no Hoko. Tokyo, 1921, p. 503.

12. Yasaburo Yoshida. "Sources and Causes of Japanese Emigration", Annals of the American Academy of Political and Social Science. Vol. 34, No. 2, Sept. 1909, p. 160.

13. Howard Sugimoto. Japanese Immigration, the Vancouver Riots and Canadian Diplomacy. University of Washington, 1966, p. 21.

14. W.L. Mackenzie King. Report of the Royal Commission Appointed to Inquire into the Methods by which Oriental Labourers have been Induced to Come to Canada. Ottawa, Government Printing Bureau, 1908, p. 5 - 6.

15. Howard Sugimoto. Japanese Immigration, the Vancouver Riots and Canadian Diplomacy. op.cit., p. 23.

16. ibid. p. 19 - 20.

17. Yasaburo Yoshida. op.cit. p. 160.

18. Rigenda Sumida. The Japanese in B.C. Vancouver, Univ. of B.C. M.A. Thesis, 1935, p. 54.

19. Junshiro Nakayama. Canada no Hoko. op.cit., p. 510 - 511.

20. ibid. p. 522.

21. W.L. Mackenzie King. op.cit., p. 32.

22. ibid., p. 33.

23. Interview with Mr. M. Kamitakahava.

24. Lethbridge Daily Herald. Apr. 26, 1908. See also Apr. 13, 1908.

25. Junshiro Nakayama. Canada no Hoko. op.cit., p. 523.

26. Lethbridge Daily Herald. Aug. 1, 1908.

27. Lethbridge Daily Herald. Nov. 12, 1908.

28. Quoted by Howard Palmer. Responses to Foreign Immigration: Nativism and Ethnic Tolerance in Alberta 1880 - 1920. op.cit., p. 206. Hereafter, "Responses to Foreign Immigration".

29. Lethbridge Daily Herald. Sept. 11, 1908.

30. Howard Palmer. Responses to Foreign Immigration. op.cit., p. 205.

31. Junshiro Nakayama. Canada no Hoko. op.cit., p. 513.

32. Interview with Giichi Tomiyama.

33. Junshiro Nakayama. Canada no Hoko. op.cit., p. 528.

34. Lethbridge Herald. Aug. 21, 1906. We are assuming that R.B. Nagatani and Takeimon Nagatani are the same persons.

35. Junshiro Nakagama. Canada no Hoko. op.cit., p. 529 - 532.

36. Canadian Japanese Assoc. The Japanese Contribution to Canada. op.cit., p. 25.

37. Lethbridge Daily Herald. Apr. 9, 1908.

38. ibid., Apr. 28, 1908.

39. ibid., Oct. 24, 1908.

40. House of Commons Debates. Jan. 28, 1908. Quoted by Howard Palmer.

41. Calgary Herald. Jan. 7, 1908.
42. Lethbridge News. Apr. 21, 1904. Also interview with Christian Peterson.
43. ibid., Sept. 18, 1906.
44. ibid., Oct. 2, 1906.
45. Lethbridge Daily Herald. Apr. 11, 1908.
46. Interview with Mr. Hisagi Sudo. Also Junshiro Nakayama, Canada no Hoko. op.cit., p. 502.
47. Interview with Hisagi Sudo and Kisaburo Sugimoto.
48. Lethbridge Daily Herald. Sept. 3, 1908.
49. Junshiro Nakayama. Canada no Hoko. op.cit., p. 503.
50. Lethbridge Daily Herald. June 8, 1908.
51. ibid., July 28, 1908.
52. See Sir Robert L. Borden. The Question of Orienta Immigration Speeches. 1908.
53. Lethbridge Daily Herald. Oct. 26, 1908.
54. Junshiro Nakayama. Canada no Hoko. op.cit., p. 505.
55. Tairiku Nippo. Canada Doho Hatten Shi. Vancouver, 1909, p. 195.
56. Junshiro Nakayama. Canada no Hoko. op.cit., p. 532.
57. Interview with M. Kamitakahara.
58. Tairiku Nippo. Canada Doho Hatten Shi. op.cit., p. 195 - 6.
59. Interview with Kaisuke Hironaka. Also Canadian Daily News. Canada Nipponjin Nogyo Hatten Go. Tokyo, 1930, p. 254.
60. Interview with Zenkitchi Shimbashi.
61. Junshiro Nakayama. Canada Doho Hatten Taikan. op.cit., p. 318.
62. Junshiro Nakayama. Canada no Hoko. op.cit., p. 1465.
63. Interview with Ito Iwaasa.
64. Interview with M. Kamitakahara.
65. Raymond Buddhist Church. A History of Forty Years of the Raymond Buddhist Church. Raymond, 1970, p. 17.

CHAPTER II   1914 - 1929

A. World War I

Cast on a small plaque attached to an aging monument for those who died in the First World War are the following words: "To the enduring memory of the men of the Raymond District who died in the Great War 1914-1918". At the bottom of a list of some ten names are listed K. Sugimoto and T. Suda. Both men were killed in action. In a letter to his brother farming in Raymond, Kitchimatsu Sugimoto wrote that he was afraid. "This war isn't like the last one (Russo-Japanese conflict). This time I'm afraid I'm going to be killed."[1] A short time later Kisaburo Sugimoto received word that his younger brother had been killed in action in France.

Besides Sugimoto and Suda, others from the Raymond district also enlisted. Among them were Hayashi, Kabachi, Kimoto, Furukawa, Okutake, and Zenkitchi Shimbashi.[2] Mr. Shimbashi relates the following experience which led to his enlistment. Apparently he went one afternoon to the movies in Lethbridge There were few people in the theatre when Lord Kitchener appeared on the screen and pointing to the audience said "You have a duty to your King and country". Mr. Shimbashi says he looked behind and there were only women. No one was beside him. Then he realized that perhaps he too was needed. A few days later while in Fort Macleod, Mr. Shimbashi, and Mr. Kimoto enlisted in the Canadian Army. From there he went to Camp Sarcee and soon after was in England.[3] The Japanese from Alberta were not confined to one particular unit and were scattered in various regiments and battalions.

An interesting sidepoint to this is that in the Fall of 1915 the Canadian Japanese Association organized the Japanese Volunteer Corps in

Vancouver. Some 202 men passed the physical examinations and they commenced training on January 17, 1916 at Cordova Hall, Vancouver. After three months of training they had still not had word from Ottawa as to their departure date so they sent a delegate to headquarters to enquire. But nothing came of the visit. However, some weeks later, a certain recruiting officer from Bremore, Alberta advised the Canadian Japanese Association that the Japanese volunteers were welcome in his battalion. After confirmation from the Canadian Government the unit left for Alberta with most of them enlisting in Calgary. The Japanese volunteers were included in the 209th Battalion; the 13th Cavalry Battalion which later became the famous Princess Patricia's; the 192nd; the 175th and 191st Battalions.[4] Mr. Shimbashi noted that about 12 Japanese from B.C. were enlisted in his unit.

Other than the two listed in Raymond as having died in action, we have no statistics as to the number of casualties from among the Southern Albertan Japanese volunteers. Since a majority of the Japanese in Southern Alberta were in essential industries such as farming and mining, conscription did not affect them very much. However, of the 197 Japanese members of the Canadian Expeditionary Force, 131 were wounded in action and 54 killed -- a moving testimony to the ferocity of the war and to the part that the Japanese played in it.[5]

Not unlike Mr. Shimbashi most of the Japanese probably enlisted because they felt that they owed a duty to Canada. A majority of them, like those who enlisted from Raymond, were Issei who had just recently taken out their naturalization papers and felt a sense of responsibility to their newly adopted country. In Japan, loyalty and responsibility had been firmly implanted in their minds during their school years, and it was quite simple to transfer this allegiance to King and country from Emperor and empire. This was especially so since Japan was also allied with Great Britain and Canada. However, there were also other less idealistic motivations which probably prompted the Japanese in Southern Alberta to enlist. Farming, mining, and railroad work usually consists of back-breaking, monotonous labour, and it is possible that the glamour of uniforms and travel appealed to not a few of the men. Many of the Japanese were either unemployed or working for very low wages, and it is not unlikely that the promise of free room and board played an important role in attracting several volunteers. Nonetheless, these same reasons played a part in everyone's decision to enlist, and the Japanese were no different from anyone else.

Once in England and in France, the Japanese often found themselves regarded as curiousities to the local inhabitants, but few experienced any overt racism. Those who could converse somewhat in English found that they were treated courteously, and made friends from among the many different nationalities in Canada's armed forces. Others who did not speak English usually kept to themselves or associated mainly with the other Japanese. However, among the soldiers there was generally a feeling of strong comradship in the face of a common enemy.

In Canada, the Japanese benefitted along with everyone else from the increased production stimulated by the war. The scarcity of labour due to the large numbers of men in the 'front', allowed the Japanese to enter several occupations that had not previously been open to them. The fact that Japan was fighting on the side of the allies tended to ease racial tensions and facilitated co-operation between racial groups.[6] In 1915, Mr. Hisagi Sudo married a white woman in Raymond and became one of the first to intermarry in Southern Alberta.[7] Bishop J. Evans of the L.D.S. Church in Raymond performed the marriage which most likely was facilitated by the easier feelings that existed between the Caucasians and the Japanese residents at this time.

With the armistice in 1918 some of this good will that had existed during the conflict disappeared. The men were back from the front and they were looking for work. The end of the war meant the end of military production quotas and the end of high prices. Influenza struck and it seemed as if the fruits of victory had been lost. Nonetheless, the good years did return and prosperity seemed just around the corner.

B. The Good Years

For the Japanese the good years stretched from 1915 to 1929. Increased production because of the war affected all of the key industries in which the Japanese were involved. Agricultural prices soared while good crops ensured a measure of prosperity never before experienced. During this period many of the bachelors decided that they needed a wife and correspondence between Japan and Canada was filled with queries and pictures.

In 1914, Mr. Kojun Iwaasa wrote back to Hiroshima giving permission to his parents to search for a wife. This most likely did not come as a surprise to his parents, since they had been urging him to do this for some time. The majority of the men in Southern Alberta. However, a certain proportion did leave their wives and children in Japan, hoping to be able to call them over as soon as they had earned enough money. On the average, this was approximately nine years after the husband arrived in Canada.[8] However, for those who were single only two options lay open to them if they were intent upon marrying a Japanese bride.[9] One option was to return to Japan and to attempt to find a wife while there on holiday, and the second option was to resort to the 'picture bride' system. If one considers the prevailing systems in Japan, the 'picture bride' system was not such a radical departure from the norm.[10] The parents would through the negotiations of a go-between (nakadoya) find a suitable bride for their son and then send a picture of the girl. If the son approved, arrangements were made, the money for the fare and western trousseau were sent by the groom and the name was entered in the prefectural records (koseki tohon). As far as the law was concerned, they were now legally married and the new bride set out to the new world to meet her husband. Sometimes they were wearing the latest styles copied from the Eaton's catalogue pages sent to them by their husbands.

In the case of Mrs. Ito Iwaasa, she was a relative of her husband whom she knew only vaguely. The arrangements for the marriage had been made by the respective parents and she had never questioned the actions. Some days prior to her departure for Canada her name was entered into the Iwaasa official records, and was officially married. She departed from Kobe in the company of Mrs. Tamaki and her child in April of 1915. Apparently, Mrs. Tamaki's husband lived near Mr. Iwaasa, and arrangements had been made through letters for the three of them to make the trip together. They met at Kobe and began the trip from there. They arrived on the 22nd of April, 1915 at Victoria. Although a great crowd awaited the arrival of the boat and nearly everyone else had someone there to meet them, no one was at the dock to meet either Mrs. Tamaki or Mrs. Iwaasa. A few days later, an apologetic Kojun Iwaasa arrived at the boardinghouse to claim his new bride and to escort Mrs. Tamaki. Because he didn't have a suit of his own, he had borrowed a suit in order to meet his bride. Thinking it wasteful to pay two fares, Mr. Tamaki had agreed to allow Mr. Iwaasa to go and bring both wives back. Mrs. Tamaki was incensed that her husband had not missed her enough to come in person to meet her at the boat after a separation of four years. Mrs. Iwaasa was incensed because he had been late to meet his new bride by some two days. On the train to Raymond, Mrs. Tamaki and Mrs. Iwaasa sat on one bench, while Mr. Iwaasa sat alone in another two or three seats back.[11]

In 1915, when Mrs. Iwaasa and Mrs. Tamaki arrived there were only five women in Raymond: Mrs. Otake, Mrs. Kuoda, Mrs. Yoichi Hironaka, and Mrs. Matsujiro Takeda, and Mrs. Tamane.[12] By 1918, five more wives had arrived in Raymond: Mrs. Koyata, Mrs. Kosaka, Mrs. Hatanaka, Mrs. Kisaburo Sugimoto, and Mrs. Tamagi.[13] The cultural shock for these new brides was very great. Often this adjustment to their new environment was complicated by the many misconceptions that many of the women had concerning Southern Alberta. Few had any conception of the vastness of the country, and the severity of the climate. When Mrs. T. Karaki arrived in Raymond she was shocked at the dark weather-beaten complexions of the Japanese who had come to the station to meet her. In fact she really wasn't sure whether they were even Japanese or not. Seeing the tiny station and the small number of houses scattered along the single main street, she assumed that the rest of the city of Raymond lay just beyond the next hill. To her disappointment, she learned that what she had seen before her was the entire town of Raymond.[14] Mrs. Sugimoto recalls crying for several days and refusing to even talk to her new husband.

Few of the Japanese had good homes and often it consisted simply of a converted granary. Mr. Sugimoto was one of the first Japanese in Raymond to purchase an old wooden frame building and remodel it into what could be described as a house. Usually these homes were situated far in the country, isolated by several miles from the nearest neighbour. Although most of these women came from farming families, the isolation and primitiveness of the accommodations was something very new to them. Mrs. Iwaasa said that her first home consisted of an old granary with a curtain in the middle to separate the kitchen from the bedroom. In order to provide more room during the day, the bed had to be rolled up and put away. During the winter the cold would penetrate the single-walled building freezing the water in the stove reservoir and making the walls white with frost. During the day, while her husband was away in the fields, she used to climb to the top of a nearby hill just to be able to see the smoke from the chimney of a neighbour some two miles away. Guests were rare during this early period and since the women could speak little, if any English, their lives were very lonely.[15]

Women often had to deliver their babies by themselves and very seldom was there any medical assistance nearby. Mrs. Iwaasa related that her husband told her to bang a big steel tub that hung outside the door with a wooden spoon when she thought that the baby was about to be delivered. This way he could hear it in the field and come to take her to the midwife. Children, however, provided welcome company for the women. Also with the children came additional opportunities to come in contact with other residents of the area. Schools provided a needed outlet for activity, not only for the children, but also for the parents.

In Raymond, the Mammoth and later the O.K. schools were simple one or two room affairs, but the large numbers of Japanese children enrolled in them made them rather unique in Southern Alberta. During picnics and sporting socials, the Japanese and Caucasian residents met and played in an atmosphere of laughter and recreation. During the late 1920's, Mr. Kojun Iwaasa became the first Japanese to serve as a school trustee in Alberta.[16]

Trustees were elected for three year terms, and Mr. Iwaasa served for two terms with such men as Golden Snow and DeLos Lund. In Hardieville, the Japanese also attended the local public schools and excelled in academic achievement.

In 1925 or 1926, Mr. C. Litchfield held night school classes at the Mammoth school for three or four young Japanese farm labourers. Many of these early school teachers played a vital role in providing the language training and social skills enabling these Japanese to integrate into Canadian society. Many of the children of these early Japanese families were also somewhat handicapped in that they did not have the opportunity of speaking English in their homes. However, in school they had the chance of mingling with Caucasian children their own ages and of developing a variety of essential socialization skills. These early one-room schools were vital in the Canadianization of the Japanese in Southern Alberta.

In 1917, the Consul-General of Japan from Vancouver, Mr. Goji Ukida, visited the area accompanied by Mr. Junshiro Nakayama.[17] Mr. Nakayama interviewed many individuals in the area and did extensive research throughout Canada which resulted in the publication of two books: Canada no Hoko and Canada Doho Hatten Taikan. These two books provide valuable insights into Japanese Canadian life during the first twenty years of the twentieth century.

In 1907, the Honourable Rodolphe Lemieux, Minister of Labour, went to Japan and negotiated a "Gentlemen's Agreement" based on a similar "Gentlemen's Agreement" negotiated in 1906 between the U.S. and Japan. According to this agreement, Japan voluntarily restricted emigration by means of two sets of regulations. The first regulation restricted Japanese emigrants to four classes: first, prior residents of Canada and their wives and children; second, those specially employed by Japanese residents in Canada for personal and domestic service; third, contract labourers whose employment was guaranteed; and fourth, agricultural labourers brought in by Japanese agricultural holders in Canada. The second regulation instructed Japanese consuls in Canada not to approve certificates for contract labourers unless these contracts received the approval of the Canadian government. Agricultural labourers were limited to ten for each one hundred acres of land owned by the Japanese in Canada. Also, no more than 400 agricultural and domestic workers were to be allowed into Canada annually.[18] In 1928, this agreement was revised, and only 150 emigrants were to be allowed to come from Japan. At this same time the "picture bride" system was also terminated.

Under these various restrictions, the Japanese farmers in Southern Alberta endeavored to bring in as many agricultural workers as possible. For this reason they co-operated in the Raymond Japanese Society, and brought in several hundred young men to assist on the farms. These men were usually either relatives or sons of friends of the family in Japan. For many, this was the only way they could hope to enter Canada. As in the case of the original pioneers these newcomers experienced the sudden change in climate and culture, but more of them were able to adapt to the new environment because they had examples of successful Japanese farmers living around them. They also had the opportunity to learn western farming methods under a type of apprenticeship system. Under this program they paid their own fare to Canada and promised to work for the farmer that sponsored them to Canada for three years. Their wages were extremely low, ranging from about $150 for the first year to about $300 for the third year. At the end of this period the men were free to establish their own farms or work elsewhere.[19]

In the coal mines at Hardieville, Coalhurst, and Diamond City, the Japanese were slowly being accepted by the other miners. None of the violent problems that had occurred in B.C. at the close of World War I happened in Southern Alberta. With the end of the war came a minor recession, but land was plentiful and so the disruption was not very large, many of the veterans going into homesteading.

There could be four reasons for this lack of conflict among the miners with the Japanese. 1) The large numbers of foreign emigrants among the miners; mostly Hungarians, Germans and Italians, made it easier for the Japanese to fit into this cosmopolitan group. 2) The fact that the Japanese were not allowed to work underground and also their comparitively few numbers meant that the Japanese did not pose a large threat to the job security of other groups. 3) The Japanese were not totally dependent on the mines for their livelihood. Many would work in the mines during the winter and then farm small acreages in the summer. Several, such as Mr. Higa and Mr. Hamabata, farmed as much as 160 acres, mostly in potatoes. 4) The Japanese were beginning to play a more active part in union affairs. Since 1909, they had been allowed to join the local mine workers' union. Mr. Chojitsu Okutake, a veteran of the First War, became an active spokesman for the Japanese in union affairs.[20]

In the 1921 Census of Canada, 473 Japanese are listed as residents of Alberta. In 1911, there had only been 247, while 1901 had recorded only 13. A tremendous upsurge in Japanese population occurred during the war period and it continued to grow during the 1920's, mostly through natural increase rather than through immigration. The 1921 Census also had an interesting break-down of the Japanese population distribution in Alberta according to

Federal Electoral Districts. The following table lists just those districts that are in Southern Alberta.

Japanese in Federal Electoral Districts

Sex	Number	Name of Federal District
Male	181	Lethbridge
Female	53	Lethbridge
Male	7	Macleod
Female	2	Macleod
Male	70	Calgary W.--O.
Female	7	Calgary W.
Male	15	Calgary E.
Female	7	Calgary E.
Male	10	Medicine Hat
Female	2	Medicine Hat
Male	13	Bow River
Female	4	Bow River

Judging from these statistics it would appear that the numbers of Japanese in Southern Alberta was definitely increasing and in 1921 was approaching 400 people. Also we can note that the bulk of the Japanese population was south of Calgary and centered around Lethbridge.

During this period from about 1920 to 1929, we begin to see a concern on the part of the Japanese in Southern Alberta for the second generation. As more and more children were being born a minor crisis occurred in the Japanese community. Concern was being expressed over the increasing westernization of the children. Many were losing their ability to express themselves in Japanese, and the further they continued on in school the worse this became. Some of the children were sent to B.C. to receive instruction in Japanese, but this soon became impractical. No doubt many wished to send their children to Japan to be educated when they became older, but this did not become as prevalent as it did in British Columbia. In about 1928, some Japanese families in Raymond decided to invite a Japanese teacher to instruct their children. Reverend Oyama, a Christian minister, was invited to come from Cumberland, B.C. to teach the children. He stayed at the Iwaasa family farm and instructed three or four children in the area. The Koyata family also played an important role in forming this embryo school. Originally it was held in the Iwaasa home but later they dragged an extra granary near the house and it acted as a school house. This only lasted for a brief period, and ceased when the Buddhist Church was formed and the minister took over the instruction on a more formal basis.[22]

During the 1920's the Japanese began to widen their social and business contacts. Cooperation between various prefectural groups increased and a greater feeling of Japanese solidarity was created. In 1914, the Japanese Society had been organized in Raymond. In 1921, the Japanese people in Hardieville also organized into the Hardieville Doshi Kai (Hardieville Friendship Society), with Mr. Shinri Higa as the first chairman. There were fifty members of the roll books and the three main objectives of the organization were as follows: 1. to promote greater cooperation among the members and to promote greater happiness for every member; 2. to assist one another to grow culturally and financially; 3. to assist those working in the mines in the case of accidents or other mutual problems.[23] The majority of the members were Okinawan miners working at #6 mine. However, miners from other prefectures were also allowed to become members and the Doshi Kai became an important social group in the Hardieville and Coaldale district. In Calgary, the Japanese had already formed the Nihonjin Kai, but during the 20's we see the formation of a "Showa Club" which was a social club organized mainly for recreation and gambling.[24] Nonetheless, the Japanese were gathering together. However, they were so scattered and their members so few that none of these groups had the power to control its members or speak in a united voice for the Japanese in Alberta in the same manner that some organizations could in B.C. Instead, the Japanese huddled together in small groups for mutual comfort.

In 1924, the Japanese in Hardieville and the Japanese in Raymond began to congregate together in the form of annual picnics. They were usually informal outings where the Okinawan Japanese and other prefectural natives could mix in a manner unheard of in Japan. Usually there was a softball or baseball game in which the two towns began to build up a lively rivalry. In Hardieville, these picnics were usually held on the Medoruma farm or the Shinei Higa farm. In Raymond, during the very early period, it was usually held on the farm of Mr. Buhatchi Nishimura who farmed with three other men six miles south-east of Raymond.[25] Occasionally, a Caucasian softball team would be challenged by the Japanese and this would be an exciting match. This was a far cry from the early reaction of many of the young Japanese workers who used to hide behind the straw-stacks in order to avoid being seen by the Caucasians for fear of being addressed, then to be unable to answer.[26]

In other areas the Japanese were beginning to diversify their occupations, and to make contacts with a wider variety of people. In Calgary, Mr. Inamasu became acquainted with Senator Pat Burns, the Alberta Cattle Baron, and as a result became the plant cook at the Burns packing plant. In 1919, Mr. Inamasu purchased the Stockyards Hotel and operated it until 1934. As his children grew older, they began to take over the cafe and hotel operations allowing Mr. Inamasu to become more and more involved in his great love of horses. He became the only Japanese racehorse trainer and owner on the North American continent.[27] In 1922, Mr. Sataro Kuwahara arrived in Calgary as the salesman for the Nikko Company selling Japanese toys and trinkets. He met Mr. Genzo Kitagawa at the Palliser Hotel, who was also a salesman. They discussed the possibility of setting up a store in the city. That Fall they opened the Nippon Bazaar, intending only to stay open until Christmas and then shut down. However, business proved to be so good that they stayed open the entire year and even began to expand. Another partner, Mr. Shinejiro Inouye was added later; the operation expanded within the city and also on to Edmonton, Regina, and Vancouver.[28]

In 1923, after a couple years of potato farming in the Raymond and Welling area, Mr. Zenkitchi Shimbashi went to work as a cook and steward at the "E.P." Ranch. This ranch was owned by the then Prince of Wales, who later became Edward VII. He was a kind man and very congenial to his employees. In 1926, when a child was born to Mr. and Mrs. Shimbashi, he gave them permission to name the child after him so the first Shimbashi child was named, 'Edward'.[29]

The Japanese were prospering and growing in numbers. Families were being born. There was greater contact among the Japanese themselves, and with the general population around them.

C. The Raymond Buddhist Church

Perhaps no single event prior to World War II had as profound an effect upon the Japanese in Southern Alberta as the formation of the Raymond Buddhist Church. Raymond became the focal point of all Japanese activities in Southern Alberta.

The Buddhist Church history, **A History of Forty Years of the Raymond**

Buddhist Church, describes the beginnings of the Japanese Buddhist Church in Raymond in the following manner:[30]

> "On July 1, 1929, the Japanese who were living in Raymond gathered at the home of Mr. Kyojun Iwasa (sic) for an O-bon-e service. The service was conducted by Reverend G. Taga, the resident minister of the Honpa Buddhist Church in Vancouver. Reverend Taga expressed his desire to see a Buddhist movement, if not a temple, established in Raymond. From this desire, the present church was established, but not without worries and efforts. With this desire, Messrs. Kyojun Iwasa, Yoshio Hatanaka, Yoichi Hironaka, Tanesaburo Kosaka, Eita Sonomura, Takejiro Koyata, Kisaburo Sugimoto, and Buhatchi Nishimura gathered their strength together to spearhead the Buddhist movement.
> Messrs. Yoichi Hironaka and Yoshio Hatanaka were elected to negotiate with the Mormon Church to purchase their building for the Buddhist Organization. As a result, the property and building were obtained for five thousand dollars."

The Raymond Japanese Society played an important part in the negotiations and was the prime mover in the establishment of the Buddhist Church in Raymond. This happened to be a very opportune time to negotiate for the former L.D.S. Church. Mr. James Walker was the Bishop of the Raymond Second Ward at the time, and he was known by both the Japanese and Caucasian residents of Raymond to be an extremely honest and fair man. As a former president of the Raymond Board of Trade and then as the Reeve of the Sugar City Municipality, James Walker was extremely respected by the Japanese. He had assisted them on many occasions to negotiate land titles and other legal matters. At this time, the Raymond Second Ward was also looking for a buyer for their church, the former white school house built in 1903. On December 15, 1928, they had begun excavations for their new church. As a result, the inquiries by Mr. Y. Hironaka and Mr. Hatanaka were given an encouraging hearing.[31]

In March of 1929, the negotiations were finally completed. On this occasion a picture was taken with many of the leading figures in the town of Raymond present. Among them were Mr. T.O. King, leading Raymond merchant;

John Evans, counsellor to the Taylor Stake Presidency; Tanesaburo Kosaka;
E. Sonomura; Takashi Karaki; T. O'Brien, former mayor of Raymond; Raymond
Knight, co-founder of Raymond; Sakutaro Saka; Joroku Akiyama; P. Cope, mayor
of Raymond; O.H. Snow, secretary-treasurer of Raymond; Kojun Iwaasa;
Takejiro Koyata; Kisaburo Sugimoto; Yoshio Hatanaka; Hikokuma Nakamura;
Toyoichi Matsuno; and Kitchinosuke Matsuyama.[32] Mr. Yoichi Hironaka is
missing from the picture. As can be easily denoted, the presence of so
many prominent individuals from the town of Raymond indicates that they were
in favour of the establishment of a Buddhist Church in town and that a very
friendly feeling existed between the two groups.

At this same time, an "Old Timer's Banquet" was held by the Japanese
in Raymond. The event was recorded in the Raymond Recorder and it notes
the attendance of many prominent individuals. The article then goes on to
state "that of the original 80 Japanese brought here as beet workers some
twenty years ago, 60 are still residents of this district. The approximate
Japanese population of the Raymond district is now about 90 adults and 94
children."[33] Mayor Cope was the after dinner speaker and he pointed out
that the Japanese citizens had been very loyal to their adopted communities.

The establishment of the Buddhist Church was the first major attempt
by the Japanese to build anything permanent in the town of Raymond itself.
Therefore, this move by the Japanese, meant that from henceforth they were
going to attempt to communicate to a greater extent with the other residents
of the community. The Japanese presence in the town of Raymond was now
firmly established.

Mr. S. Motoyama, a carpenter by trade, directed the remodelling of the
interior of the old building. Most of the labour was donated, but finances
still proved to be a very serious problem. Money was needed to pay for the

building and for the remodelling expenses. As a consequence, a 'hundred year plan' was organized in which individuals pledged various amounts of money. One hundred and twenty-four people pledged some seven thousand three hundred and eighty-seven-dollars. This was an extremely large sum, if one takes into consideration the date (1929) and the financial position of the Japanese in the area.[34]

With the assistance of REverend Taga in Vancouver, a minister direct from University in Japan, Reverend Shinjo Nagatomi was retained. He arrived in Raymond on June 4, 1930. That summer a huge welcome picnic was held on the farm of Mr. Ei Sonomura in his new barn. Japanese residents from Hardieville, Coalhurst, Raymond, and other surrounding areas in Southern Alberta gathered. What had been held on rather an informal basis became an institution among the Japanese and annual picnics were held until after World War II.[35]

The first services were held in the new Buddhist Church on March 23, 1929.[36] It is interesting to note that the formation of the Raymond Buddhist Church made news in other areas. Cynthia Carghill wrote an article in 1931 entitled "Japanese in South of Province Making Good" in the Alberta Farmer.[37] This same article appeared in the Calgary Herald.

Times were changing for the Japanese. Their children were growing up, and financially they were becoming more and more independent with larger farms and new equipment. The Japanese were now participating, albeit on a limited scale, as members of a larger community. The ideals expressed in the constitution of the Raymond Japanese Society in 1914 were being fulfilled. However, despite the apparent success of the early Japanese residents, troubles darkened the future and the embryo Buddhist Church was to play a crucial role in the developments of the future.

FOOTNOTES

1. Interview with Kiseburo Sugimoto.

2. Interviews with Hisogi Sudo and Zonkitchi Shimbashi. Some of these men may not have been residents of Southern Alberta prior to enlisting.

3. Interview with Zenkitchi Shimbashi.

4. Canadian Japanese Assoc. The Japanese Contribution to Canada. op.cit., p. 41 - 42.

5. ibid. p. 42.

6. Charles H. Young; Helen R.Y. Reid; and W.A. Carrothers. The Japanese Canadians. Toronto, Univ. of Toronto Press, 1938, p. 128.

7. Interview with Hisagi Sudo.

8. Charles H. Young, et.al. The Japanese Canadians. op.cit., p. 88.

9. ibid. p. 94. Few men contemplated inter-marriage.

10. ibid. p. 15. See C.J. Woodsworth. Canada and the Orient. op.cit., p. 94.

11. Interview with Ito Iwaasa.

12. Interview with Ito Iwaasa.

13. Interview with Kaisuke Hironaka.

14. Interview with Mrs. T. Karaki.

15. Interview with Ito Iwaasa.

16. Interview with Orin Turner and Golden Snow.

17. Interview with Takayuki Kubota.

18. Charles H. Young, et.al. The Japanese Canadians. op.cit., p. 10 - 16.

19. Interview with Takayuki Kubota and Mitsuo Karaki.

20. Interview with Sucho Higa.

21. Sixth Census of Canada, 1921. Vol. I, Ottawa, King's Printer, 1924.

22. Interview with Tadao Iwaasa.

23. Rollaand minute books of the Hardieville Doshi Kai, owned by Mr. Sucho Higa.

24. Interviews with Mrs. S. Kuwahara, and Miss Mary Inamasu.
25. Interviews with Sucho Higa, Ito Iwaasa, Takayuki Kubota, and Mitsuo Karaki.
26. Interview with Takayuki Kubota.
27. Winnipeg Free Press. Oct. 25, 1958. Also interview with Mary Inamasu.
28. Nihon Sangyo Kyokai. Dai Jusanji: Sangyo Bocki Korosha Shoseki Ryoku. Tokyo, 1936, p. 37. Interview with Mrs. S. Kuwahara.
29. Hiroto Takemi. Canada no Nihonjin. Tokyo, 1969, p. 148 - 150. Interview with enkitchi Shimbashi.
30. Raymond Buddhist Church. A History of Forty Years of the Raymond Buddhist Church. Raymond, 1970, p. 140.
31. J.O. Hicken (compiler). Raymond Roundup. Raymond, 1967, p. 129 - 130, p. 113 and p. 287 - 289.
32. J.O. Hicken (compiler). Raymond Roundup. op.cit., p. 130.
33. Raymond Recorder. Mar. 16, 1929.
34. Raymond Buddhist Church. A History of Forty Years of the Raymond Buddhist Church. op.cit., p. 139.
35. ibid. p. 133 and an interview with Takayuki Kubota.
36. Lethbridge Herald. Mar. 26, 1969.
37. Cynthia Carghill. "Japanese in Southeof Province Making Good", Alberta Farmer. Dec. 17, 1931.
38. Calgary Herald. Dec. 5, 1931.

CHAPTER III   1929 - 1941

   A. The Bad Years

The 1930's brought something the early Japanese were very familiar with - drought. Money was scarce and markets fell drastically. However, this time the Japanese could not move on. Their families were growing, and they had large investments in land and equipment. The contract farm labourers had stopped coming since 1928, but now the earlier ones were beginning to start farming on their own. Those who could, no doubt, did move on -- back to Japan or to B.C. But for most of the Japanese there was no choice but to stay. The drought emphasized the importance of having irrigated land; and as new areas were opened up to irrigation, the Japanese moved to them.

The Depression brought new stresses into consideration, but in many ways relations between the Japanese and white residents in the Raymond district improved. Both groups were experiencing the same difficulties, and neighbours had to come closer together in order to survive. The children were becoming friends in school, and this encouraged social contact between the two groups. However, in the cities and other industrial areas, these new economic stresses placed an added difficulty upon the Japanese. Like other workers dependent upon unskilled labour jobs, the Japanese found themselves unemployed. In Hardieville, the mines closed down and the Japanese were forced to find other means of employment. Most of the men owned small farms and they returned to farming full time. The Doshi Kai became the Lethbridge Nokai or Agricultural Society.[1]

At this time, ominous things were happening in B.C. and some of the anti-Asiatic agitation entered into Alberta. The local papers often carried news releases from Vancouver, and Southern Alberta residents were well aware of the developments in British Columbia and California. In May of 1930, Charles E. Hope of the White Canada Association wrote a letter to Premier J.E. Brownlee of Alberta advocating that the four western provinces adopt the same policy regarding provincial voters lists.[2] By this, Mr. Hope was asking Alberta to adopt a policy already in force in B.C. since 1895 that denied the franchise to all Orientals.[3] Alberta had no discriminatory legislation against Orientals; and since Premier Brownlee took no action on Mr. Hope's suggestions, no changes were made. Some other organizations expressed sympathy with the White Canada Association. These were the Trade & Labour Congress of Canada, the United Farmers of Alberta, and the Great War Veterans Association.[4]

However, it was the sugar beet industry that was once again to need the Japanese. In 1925, when the Alberta Sugar Beet Growers Association was formed, a resolution was passed in one of their first meetings stating that rather than bring in Oriental laouur they would bring in Europeans.[5] Various problems occurred later that forced them to reverse that decision. In 1935, the Picture Butte Sugar Factory was put into operation, and sugar beets were in great supply. It was then that a major portion of the sugar beet workers went on strike. After considerable negotiations, the strike was finally settled on May 27, 1936. Nonetheless, this incident created a great deal of distrust between the Eastern European beet workers and the sugar beet growers. One of the notices placed by the Alberta Beet Workers' Union, which had organized the strike, went like this:

> "Fellow Workers: The Beet Workers' Union in process of negotiations with the Beet Growers' Association and the Canadian Sugar Factories Co. Ltd., against slave conditions and a system of piece work which compels workers to slave sixteen hours daily for at best fifteen to twenty cents an hour, calls on all workers to stay from the beet fields of Southern Alberta.

>Bosses fearing strike are undertaking to import workers
>to discriminate against union members in an effort to discredit
>and break the Beet Workers' Union.
>
>The beet growers at Diamond City apparently are not taking
>us very seriously. They have decided to ignore the demands of
>the Beet Workers and hire scab labor form among the Jap miners
>at No. 6 mine, if a report we have received from a Diamond Beet
>Grower is correct."

As we can see from this public notice put up by the Beet Workers' Union, local 103, once again the Japanes were caught in between two groups in a violent labour dispute.

Even though this dispute was eventually solved, the situation worsened; and in 1941, another strike was called by the Beet Workers' Union. The main demands were a contract demanding $9.00 per acre for thinning and recognition of the grievance committee of the Alberta Workers' Union by the Alberta Co-operative Beet Growers' Association. It was on the recognition portion that the Beet Growers and the Factory balked at. Evidence of this situation occurred when Mr. Phil Baker, president of the Beet Growers' Association, was invited to attend a public meeting sponsored by the Alberta Beet Workers' Union on July 7, 1941. The Honorable J.H. Blackmore, M.P. and Roy S. Lee, M.L.A. were slated to speak there. In a letter dated July 2, 1941, Mr. T. George Wood, District Manager of the Canadian Sugar Factories Ltd., advised Mr. Phil Baker in the following manner:

>"It seems to me that the directors of the Beet Growers'
>Association are out of place in a meeting called by the Beet
>Workers' Union."

Obviously, the Factory did not want any recognition of collective bargaining to be given.

The workers were also exploiting an excellent situation. The was had drained a great percentage of the available manpower away from the area. According to the Federal Department of Agriculture, Alberta had lost some

23.9% of her farm labour source in 1940, and by 1941 this had become 43.9%.

Net Loss of Labour per 100 Farms

Year	Canada	Alberta	Manitoba	Ontario	B.C.
1940	21.6	23.9	31.6	21.7	17.2
1941	34.5	43.9	44.1	32.2	29.9

Source: Dept. of Agriculture. "Farm Labour in Wartime", Ottawa, 1943, Table #5.

Coupled with this, the amount of sugar needed for the war effort had increased drastically. Some additional 4000 acres were required. The local workers knew that there was no additional source of labour in sight and were anxious to have their demands met while they were in this favourable position. It was into this volatile situation that the Japanese entered into in 1942.

During the 30's, the Japanese from Raymond began to branch out into the surrounding districts. Often they did not find a welcome response to their coming, but as they established themselves and proved to the community that they were honest and responsible citizens, the hostility turned to tolerance and sometimes even acceptance as friends and neighbours. Some moved to Fort Macleod and started market gardening there.[9] In 1933, Mr. Kahei Sawada went to Pincher Creek as a barber, having barbered in both Raymond and Lethbridge.[10] The 1930's saw the beginning of the movement of Japanese to the Rosemary and Duchess area. Irrigation had been introduced and land was inexpensive. Mr. Kaisuke Hironaka was one of the first Japanese residents in the area, pioneering the potato industry. Soon other Japanese in search of cheap irrigated land moved up to the area. Among these was the Ohama family who soon became one of the larger potato farmers in the province. Since the numbers of Japanese in these areas were very small, they were eventually able to mix well with the local residents. In Calgary,

Kumataro Inamasu's horse, the Duchess of York, was making headlines as she won races in the United States and Canada. In a small way, the Japanese in Alberta were becoming better known.[11]

In Raymond, the Buddhist Church was becoming more firmly established. Reverend Shinjo Nagatomi, the first minister, arrived on June 4, 1930. A short time later, his wife arrived and began to teach Japanese school lessons to the local Japanese children. The parents were anxious to have the children learn Japanese so that they could communicate better. Most of the children were forgetting what Japanese they had known prior to attending public school. As a result, the Buddhist ministers played a vital role in attempting to preserve the Japanese language and culture among the local residents. Following Reverend Nagatomi, Reverend Yutetsu Kawamura arrived on July 5, 1934. He remained until January 13, 1940. During Reverend Kawamura's ministry we see the Buddhist Church spread throughout Southern Alberta. He made periodic visits as far north as Calgary. The Japanese began to look to Raymond increasingly as the centre of Japanese culture in Southern Alberta. The annual Buddhist festivals such as "Hanamatsuri" in April and "O-bon-e" service held in July became occasions on which Japanese throughout Southern Alberta would gather to renew old acquaintances and make new ones. These religious festivals and the annual Japanese picnics served to cement the Japanese closer together. It was not, however, a restrictive type of situation, because on these occasions both Christian and Buddhist Japanese could gather together in a spirit of fellowship.[12]

Politically, the Japanese in the Raymond District, had not been very active. In 1940, however, many Japanese supported James H. Walker in his successful bid for a seat in the provincial legislature as a member of the Independent Party. Party affiliations and other political factors had little to do with the gaining of the Japanese support. They voted for the man. James Walker had been fair with them in the past and they saw no reason why he would not be equally as fair in Edmonton. Integrity was more important than platform. Many of the Japanese felt that they owed "giri" to Mr. Walker because of the many services that he had performed for them in the past. This sense of moral obligation or "giri" as it is called in Japanese, was very strong among the early Japanese residents, and her again we see examples of 'old world' values being applied by the Japanese in a 'new world' situation.

B. The Manchurian Crisis and War in China

In September of 1931, the so-called 'Manchurian Incident' plunged the armies of Japan into an all-out fight to conquer all of Manchuria for Japan. Within a few months Manchuria had been overrun. Finally in 1932, the Japanese made Manchuria into the puppet state of 'Manchukuo'. Canada, along with other members of the League of Nations expressed strong disapproval on this outburst of military aggression, but was also equally unwilling to do anything positive about it. In July of 1937, after another 'incident' in Peking, the Japanese army initiated an attempt to conquer all of China.[1]

Reaction in Canada was spotty. Those who were knowledgeable about the situation condemned the actions and attempted to create some public opinion against Japan. White extremists in British Columbia seized upon the Chinese conflict to vilify the Japanese in Canada once more. However, reaction in Southern Alberta was generally one of disinterest. China seemed far away, and the economic problems at home seemed much more pressing. Incidents such as the 'rape of Nanking' received considerable press coverage, and a few isolated incidents of ill-feelings towards the Japanese in Alberta

did occur. The interesting development concerning this is that it was the
Chinese who began to condemn the Japanese the most. In Calgary, the Chinese
restaurant and grocery operators refused to serve Japanese customers. Some
were forced to turn away their long-time Japanese customers because of
social pressures placed upon them by other members of the Chinese community.[14]
In Lethbridge also, isolated incidents occurred where Chinese restaurants
would not serve Japanese. In one incident, some very angry Chinese even
picketted the Silk-o-lina Shop in Calgary, owned by the Kuwahara family,
pointing at them and calling them 'Japs'.[15] The Chinese went to great eff
to identify themselves as being different than the Japanese. In 1939, when
Canada went to war against Germany, greater efforts were made by the Chinese
community to get the allies involved against another aggressor, Japan.

C. War with Germany

In September of 1939, Canada declared war on Germany and embarked on
a hazardous journey. Public support for the war was almost unanimous, with
only one dissenting voice in the House of Commons. Generally, the Japanese
in Canada were at one with the rest of the citizens of Canada and supported
the move. Some of the Issei, however, expressed reservations concerning
the war and the increased nationalistic and 'jingoistic' fervor generated
by the war effort. On the other hand, the Nisei were soon caught up in the
enthusiasm to enlist and saw this as an opportunity to demonstrate their
loyalty to Canada.

1940 saw the situation become somewhat more complex. The war was
not going well for the allies. The National Resources Mobilization Act was
brought forward in the House of Commons and the entire nation was put on a
war footing. Conscription was again being debated and W.L. Mackenzie King

vacillated. On October 1, 1940, the Cabinet War Committee appointed a special committee to investigate the situation concerning persons of Japanese and Chinese racial origin living in B.C. The three members of this committee were: Lt.-Col. A.W. Sparling, convener; Dr. H.L. Keenleyside; and Assistant Commissioner F.J. Mead of the R.C.M.P. On September 27, the Japanese had signed the Tripartite Alliance with Germany and Italy, becoming one of the Axis powers. Many Japanese in Canada expressed concern over this move by Japan, but again they were helpless to do anything about it.[16] One of the duties of the Special Committee on Orientals in B.C. was as follows:[17]

> "To consider in particular what steps should be taken in regard to the application to oriental Canadians of the terms of the National Resources Mobilization Act, 1940."

It is interesting to note the manner in which they stated their conclusion. Only points 36 and 37 are relevant to our discussion.[18]

> "Coming finally to the problem of compulsory military training for Canadian citizens of Japanese race, the Committee are agreed that all Canadian citizens, irrespective of race, in principle possess all the rights and duties of citizenship, and that therfore citizens of Japanese race can claim the right to be given military training and to serve in the armed forces...Many Japanese Canadians have in fact expressed their desire to serve, and some have definitely stated that they were even prepared to fight against other Japanese in the unhappy event of war against Japan.
> Although the members of the Committee sympathize with this attitude, they are bound to consider the question in relation to other facts, and those facts are that opinion in B.C. is on the whole against allowing persons of Japanese race to take military training, or to serve in the armed forces...a more valid objection was raised by those who urged that, particularly in the event of increased tension between Japan and the democratic states, the situation of Japanese Canadian youths in training or serving in military units with large numbers of white Canadians would be one of great danger should racial or national passion be aroused by some untoward incident at home or abroad...Therefore, it has been decided to recommend, though most reluctantly and not unanimously, that at least for the present, Canadians of Japanese race should not be given military training (except of course the Basic Training provided for all students in public schools and universities) and should not be enlisted generally in the armed forces of Canada."

Generally speaking, this recommendation seems to have been adhered to in regards to enlistment of Japanese in B.C. However, this was not true in other areas of the country. The ironic thing is that while Japanese Canadians in B.C. were being rejected or discouraged from enlisting, Japanese Canadians in Alberta and other areas of Canada were being accepted without any difficulties.[19]

During 1940 and 1941, the following individuals enlisted in the Canadian armed forces from Southern Alberta: from Raymond--Toru Iwaasa, Scotty Oshiro Joe Takahashi, and Shin Takahashi; from Hardieville and Coaldale--Harry Higa, Tom Matsuoka, and George Higa who was a member of the reserve army until 1944 when he was called to serve in Burma; and from Calgary--Harry Inamasu (Jim Inamasu was conscripted but served for only a few months). Three of the Raymond boys joined the 6th Field Park of the Royal Canadian Engineers which was formed in Lethbridge.[20] Joe Takahashi joined the Calgary Highlanders and became one of the very few, if not the only, Japanese Canadian in a Highland Regiment. Therefore, conditions were obviously not uniform throughout the Dominion.

Starting in March of 1941, under Orders-in-Council P.C. 117 and 9760, all Japanese in Canada were registered by the Canadian Mounted Police.[21] Apparently, this registration also took place in Southern Alberta, although most Japanese residents of Southern Alberta during this time either do not recall anything or have only a vague recollection of having been visited by the R.C.M.P. once during the war. However, this was carried out and some 534 Japanese were registered as being resident in Alberta as of January 1, 1942. This registration was carried out by the R.C.M.P. officers within the area. No doubt this action by the Dominion Government would have disturbed the local Japanese residents, but it was carried out in an extremely efficient and unobtrusive manner by the Mounted Police and few individuals were even aware that it was taking place. Registration cards which include a picture and other identifying information were not handed out as they were in B.C. Again the Japanese in Southern Alberta were treated somewhat differently than those in British Columbia.

D. Pearl Harbour

On the morning of December 7, 1941, Japanese bombers attacked Pearl Harbour and in one blow virtually eliminated the United States Pacific Fleet as a fighting unit. The world listened in stunned amazement as the first reports of this victory for Japan cam crackling over the short-wave radios. It seemed as if the Japanese would be on the doorsteps of every home in North America within the week, as news of the crippling of the largest navy in the Pacific became known.

The reaction of the Japanese in Canada to the news of Japan's attack on Pearl Harbour was one of equal shock and amazement. Many heard the news of Japan's victory over the Japanese short-wave broadcasts from Tokyo. Those who could read or understand English learned of the news in the ordinary manner. Mr. Kaisuke Hironaka recalls that his Caucasian neighbour came over and told him about it, reassuring him that it wouldn't make any difference in their relationship. Among the Japanese there was basically three different reactions to the news. A small group of the Japanese were actually in favour of the Japanese move. In B.C. this group had some very vocal advocates and in many ways caused some of the fear and anxiety already felt by many of the local white residents. In Alberta this group was much less vocal, but nonetheless, they existed. For the most part, the most recently arrived Issei were in this category. There was another group which included almost all of the second generation Japanese and a good proportion of the first generation. Somewhat larger in number than the first group, this group actively opposed the Japanese action and advocated loyalty to Canada.[23] The third group, which was composed of the majority of the Issei and a certain proportion of the Nisei, was confused and apprehensive of the future. Although this group was opposed to the actions of the Japanese military, they could not identify Japan as an enemy. Usually this group was swayed by whomever of the other two groups sounded the most convincing in the light of the circumstances. As persecution from official sources increased, some sided with the pro-Japanese clique. But the majority remained confused and wished to maintain the good graces of both factions. It is highly probable that had the Canadian government come out with a definite statement concerning the status of the Japanese in Canada, resasuring them and promising just treatment as Canadian citizens, a majority of the Japanese would have sided with those advocating loyalty to Canada. However, the vacillating actions of the Dominion Government and their apparent branding of all Japanese as enemy aliens irregardless of citizenship, caused anxiety and insecurity among the Japanese in B.C. and to some extent among the Japanese in Southern Alberta.

In Southern Alberta, the more prominent members of the Japanese community came out in public support of loyalty to Canada. Yoichi (Harry) Hironaka, Shinei Higa, and Kojun (Henry) Iwaasa along with a majority of the older Japanese residents of the area spoke out against the Japanese military action. Some thirty years after the event, one Japanese resident who was present at the time, said that after having travelled through a good portion of North America and having seen the vastness of the country, he knew that Japan could never win the war. Others advocated loyalty for more pragmatic reasons, but nonetheless, only a small minority in Southern Alberta seemed to sympathize with Japan. Since most of the sanctions imposed upon the Japanese in B.C., such as the impounding of radios and automobiles, did not apply to those who had resided in Alberta prior to 1942, the pro-Japanese faction did not grow in size, but rather diminished as the tide of the war turned against Japan.

As for those already serving in the Canadian armed forces, news of Pearl Harbour came as a surprise as it did to most everyone else. But there were none of the incidents feared by the Special Committee on Orientals. In fact in many incidents, Caucasian soldiers went out of their way to be more pleasant to the Japanese, and sometimes they would come up and reassure their Japanese comrades that war with Japan made no difference in their personal relationships.

The Caucasian population of Southern Alberta never agitated for expulsion or other restrictions. They never looked upon their Japanese residents as potential subversives in the same way as the residents of B.C. did. However, as the war progressed, feelings did become somewhat strained and often people forgot that there had been a distinction made at the beginning between the local Japanese residents and those Japanese who lived on the coast. Personal prejudices surfaced and people made public statements that they had felt for many years but had never dared utter before. Events in B.C. and in California were carefully reported in the local newspapers and many people had relatives and friends living on the coast. Most of the popular rumours and misconceptions prevalent on the coast also found their way into gossip sessions and luncheon discussions throughout Southern Alberta. However, for those local residents who had been familiar with the Japanese for many years, either as business associates or as neighbours, the war actually brought little change in their usually congenial relationships.

FOOTNOTES

1. Interview with Sucho Higa.

2. *Premier's Papers*, Provincial Archives of Alberta, Edmonton, Alberta.

3. Charles J. Woodsworth. *Canada and the Orient*. op.cit., p. 42.

4. Patricia E. Roy. "The Oriental Problem in the Inter-War Years", *British Columbia's Campaign for a 'White Canada'*. University of Victoria, 1972.

5. O.S. Longman (Research officer). *The Beet Sugar Industry in Alberta*. Glenbow Foundation Project, 1960, p. 464.

6. *Alberta Sugar Beet Growers' Assoc. Papers*. Glenbow Alberta Institute Library, Calgary, Alberta.

7. ibid.

8. Kimiaki Nakashima. *Economic Aspects of the Japanese Evacuation from the Canadian Pacific Coast*. Montreal, McGill Univ. M.A. Thesis, 1946, p. 19.

9. Interview with Giichi Tomiyama.

10. Interview with Kaisuke Hironaka.

11. *Calgary Daily Herald*. Oct. 11, 1930.

12. Raymond Buddhist Church. *A History of Forty Years of the Raymond Buddhist Church*. op.cit., p. 133.

13. Edwin O. Reischauer. *Japan: Past and Present*. Tokyo, Charles E. Tuttle, 1967, p. 186 - 189.

14. Interviews with Kaisuke Hironaka and Mrs. S. Kuwahara.

15. Interview with Hiroshi Kuwahara.

16. Interview with Mrs. K. Sawada.

17. Canada. Special Committee on Orientals in B.C. *Report and Recommendations, Dec. 1940*. Ottawa, 1941, p. 2.

18. ibid., p. 14.

19. See H. Norman. *What About the Japanese Canadians?* Vancouver, Consultative Council for Cooperation in Wartime Problems of Canadian Citizenship, 1945, p. 12.

20. Interview with Toru Iwaasa.

21. Canada. Dept. of Labour. *Report on Administration of Japanese Affairs in Canada, 1942-44.* op.cit., p. 2.

22. Interviews, and ibid. p. 2.

23. See *Lethbridge Herald*, December 12, 1941 the article "Jap Canadian Vets Pledge Loyalty in New War as in First Great War."

CHAPTER IV   1941 - 1945

A. The 'Old-timers'

According to the 1945 Census of Canada, there were 578 persons of Japanese racial origin in the Province of Alberta. Of these, there were probably no more than 100 who were not living in Southern Alberta. Census district #2 which included the Raymond and Lethbridge area had 346 Japanese residents within its boundaries alone, and there were some 50 Japanese in the city of Calgary which would bring the total close to 400. For the most part, these were individuals and their descendants who had come to Alberta prior to the Second World War. They were the old-timers' and they were to play an important role in the subsequent drama that was to follow.

Although some bitterness had occurred in the very early period when the Japanese had first arrived in Southern Alberta, racial discrimination and racial hatred were distant forces to most Southern Albertan Japanese. Most of the Japanese and their children were beginning to acculturate very well into the local communities. They were 'just neighbours' and nothing else as far as most individuals were concerned. Pearl Harbour had jeopardized this comfortable position, and the Japanese in Southern Alberta were anxious to demonstrate their loyalty. On December 8, the day after Pearl Harbour, a huge article appeared in the Lethbridge Herald under the following heading, "Many Alta. Japs are Naturalized Canadian Citizens".[1] The article goes on to state that there were between 250 and 260 Japanese centered chiefly in Raymond. It also states that "some time ago the Japanese residents were registered and numbers of them fingerprinted by the Mounted Police."[2] The local correspondent stated that it was expected that the Japanese aliens would be interned, similar to the nationals of other enemy countries.[3] Part of the article was entitled "Loyalty Voiced" and contained the following:[4]

> "South Alta. Japanese leaders have avowed their loyalty to Canada and the actual declaration of war and armed action by Japan came as a shock to them. A number of Raymond Japanese are in the Canadian army."

The same article chronicled briefly the history of the Japanese in the Raymond district. Harry (Yoichi) Hironaka was quoted as saying:

> "There are about 40 of the Japanese colony old-timers still living in the Raymond District. We have been here many years, raised our families here, own property here. This is our home. We are behind Canada one hundred percent and have supported the Red Cross and other war efforts. We will continue that support and if necessary fight for Canada."

The local Japanese were very anxious to establish their loyalty.

Six days after Pearl Harbour, the following article appeared in the Lethbridge Herald:[5]

"Japanese Help Red Cross; Pledge Complete Loyalty"

> "Pledging their loyalty to Canada, Japanese residents of Lethbridge and district on Friday made a contribution of $90 to the Canadian Red Cross. They expressed, through George Higa, a member of the Canadian Reserve Army, whose brother Harry Higa is with the Canadian Forces overseas, their disapproval of the action of the Japanese militarists in bringing on the present war in the Pacific...
> Even before the war broke out in the Pacific they state they heartily disliked the attitude of the Japanese military party in the Orient and they were hopeful of a peaceful settlement between the Japanese, American and British governments. The declaration of war took them by surprise."

This same article goes on to give a pledge of loyalty given on behalf of the Japanese in the district:

> "Each and every resident here of Japanese descent pledge their loyalty to Canada and wish to cooperate with their fellow Canadians in any endeavour to achieve ultimate victory. Even before the Hawaiian episode some of the Japanese youths had enlisted in the active forces. Two of them, Harry Higa and Tom Matsuoka are overseas with the Canadian Army, the former with the Ordance Corps and the latter with the Engineers. There are many who state they wish to enlist after Christmas and New Year's. Their ancestors were warriors in Japan, therefore these youths are expected to perform their duty with the same spirit of their ancestors, they stated."

Since the Japanese attack on Pearl Harbour, nearly every edition of the local press carried articles concerning Japanese advance in China and in the various South Sea islands. December 10 saw the sinking of the H.M.S. Prince of Wales and the H.M.S. Repulse. Then on December 25, Hong Kong fell and some 2000 Canadian soldiers who had been stationed there were either killed or captured. Although one could not describe the general atmosphere as one of panic, the newspaper articles do indicate a feeling of anxiety and apprehension concerning the future of the war in the Pacific. The situation appeared to be going from bad to worse. In the light of these incidents and the ominous news from British Columbia, one cannot blame the local Japanese residents for being somewhat over anxious to prove their loyalty.

The Chinese residents of the district were jubilant that the United States had commenced hostilities with Japan. A spokesman for the Lethbridge Chinese made the following statement that was quoted by the Lethbridge Herald:[7]

> "Japan will be brought to justice for its mass murders of helpless Chinese women and children during the past few years. With the United States fighting with us, we'll be able to eat the Japs."

Obviously there was no love lost between the local Chinese and Japanese residents with the beginning of hostilities. Ever since the Sino-Japanese War that ended in defeat for China in 1895, the Japanese and Chinese had been archrivals. Emigration to Canada lessened this feeling somewhat, but other deep-seated differences still existed and the two Oriental communities had never been completely at ease with each other. The Manchurian and Chinese conflicts had intensified these feelings, and many Japanese in Southern Alberta commented that although white restaurant owners and hotel-keepers continued to serve Japanese during the war on an almost unchanged basis, most Chinese restaurants in both Lethbridge and Calgary had refused to serve

Japanese.[8] It is apparent from this that the white population was more willing to accept the concept that Japanese residents in Canada were now Canadians than were the Chinese residents.

One group very often missed in discussions concerning Japanese Canadians is that of these born in Canada but educated in Japan. Although there were probably several, we are only aware of three in Southern Alberta. One was the son of Mr. Yoichi Hironaka, Aki, who studied in Japan just prior to the war and was able to return to Canada before the outbreak of hostilities with the U.S. Another individual by the name of Nishio went to Japan from Calgary and was conscripted in Japan, but managed to return unharmed. The saddest case is that of Mitsuo Kuwahara who went to Japan in 1939 to learn Japanese. He was enrolled in Keio University when he was conscripted for the Japanese army. He was sent to Saipan where he met his death.[9]

The Caucasian residents of Southern Alberta had mixed feelings toward the local Japanese residents. The early newspaper articles were all very quick to point out that the Japanese to whom they were referring had been in Alberta for several decades. Perhaps of all the areas in Southern Alberta, the feeling in Raymond was the most congenial. On January 2, 1942, a banquet was held in Raymond for three of the four local Japanese youths serving with the Canadian forces. Home on leave were Toru Iwaasa, Scotty Oshiro, and Shin Takahashi. Mr. Henry (Kojun) Iwaasa, who presided over the meeting, was described as "a leading Japanese personality who has resided here for more than three decades." In attendance were most of the town's leading white residents. James H. Walker, M.L.A. for the Warner constituency spoke at the meeting and was quoted in the following manner:[10]

> "James H. Walker, M.L.A., spoke of the Raymond Japanese people, whom he said were most honorable and law-abiding citizens, and said it was regrettable that Japan should have started a war on the

democracies. He paid tribute to the loyalty of Raymond's Japanese in supporting and cooperating in any civic project undertaken by Raymond. Mr. Walker reminded his naturalized Japanese listeners that they were entitled to and would share equal privileges with other citizens of Canada, irregardless of creed or color."

Mayor Cope of Raymond and Sergeant Major Dyson made similar statements quoted in the same article. However, there were no doubt a great many individuals who had misgivings about the Japanese living around them and felt that certain restrictions should be placed on them. This reaction became more pronounced as the B.C. evacuees came into the area. Frequently, the restrictions placed upon the evacuees were applied in such a manner that it did not seem mo matter whether one had been a resident of Southern Alberta prior to 1942 or not. In fact, as more and more Japanese began to move in from the coast, many local residents were oblivious to the fact that Japanese had been living in Southern Alberta since 1905 and that no terrible consequences had resulted. Although most of the individuals who had been responsible for the evacuation of the coastal Japanese to Southern Alberta were aware of the important influence exerted by the 'old timers' among the Japanese in advocating loyalty to Canada, the war had placed all Japanese under suspicion. The 1942 evacuation changed the lives of not only the evacuees, but also the lives of the local white and Japanese residents in Southern Alberta.

B. The Evacuees

1. The Sugar Beet Fields Again

One of the recommendations of the Special Committee on Orientals in B.C. was that a Standing Committee on Orientals be appointed. This was done and Mayor Fred J. Hume of New Westminster served as Chairman with Lt.-Col. Sparling, Assistant Commissioner Mead of the R.C.M.P., Professor H.F. Angus of U.B.C., and Lt.-Col. MacGregor MacIntosh of the B.C. Legislature as members of the committee. It was to this group that the first inquiries concerning the possible use of Japanese workers in the sugar beet fields were made. Among the various clippings in the files of the Alberta Sugar Beet Growers' Association is a Herald clipping dated January 5 that is headlined "Committee on Jap Situation Goes to Ottawa."[11] In this article is the following:

> "Vancouver newspapers said the committee was recommending that all Japanese of whom there are some 24,000 be placed in camps and where they possibly could be formed into labor corps...."

Possibly motivated by the potential of such a labor corps in solving the chronic labour difficulties experienced by the sugar beet growers, on January 28, 1942, W.F. Russell, secretary of the Alberta Sugar Beet Growers' Association, wrote a letter to Mayor Hume enquiring about the possibility of employing Japanese workers in Southern Alberta.[12] It is uncertain as to what the immediate reply was, but on February 17, 1942, Mr. A. MacNamara, Associate Deputy Minister of Labour, wrote the following:[13]

> "Unofficial advice has been placed in my hands to the effect that the Alberta Sugar Beet Growers' Association is somewhat interested in obtaining the assistance of Japanese labour in connection with the cultivation of sugar beets...Japanese Nationals, who are men born in Japan and enemy aliens, as well as Canadians of Japanese racial origin born in Canada are available...It strikes me that it might be possible for your Association to work out some mutually satisfactory arrangement for the employment of this surpluss labour."

It wasn't until February 26, 1942, that the plans for complete evacuation of the Japanese from the 'protected areas' of B.C. were announced. Obviously, plans were being considered for removal of the Japanese 'surplus labour' much prior to that time.

Southern Alberta had always been plagued with a shortage of labour. The sugar beet fields especially were beginning to feel the drain of labour to the war industries in the cities and into the armed forces. Alberta had lost some 23.9% of her farm labour in 1940, and by 1941 this had grown to some 43.9%.[14] The Alberta Sugar Beet Growers' Association was confronting various labour problems and the Beet Workers' Union composed mostly of Hungarians were making various demands on the growers to improve working conditions and wages. As a consequence, the farmers were quick to seize upon any opportunity to relieve this perennial problem.

It is quite likely that the proposal to bring the Japanese into the sugar beet fields originated in one of the locals of the Sugar Beet Growers' Association, either in Picture Butte, Raymond, or Taber. It was obviously much debated before the Board approved some tentative investigations.[15] They knew that labour was desperately needed. The Japanese had truck farming experience and were known to be diligent workers. There really was not much choice, and in many ways this was a 'windfall' for the beet growers.[16] Evidence of some very early sentiment was expressed in a telegram sent to Gordon L. Smith of the *Financial Post* in Toronto from P.T. Rogers in Raymond.[17]

> "This area in Southern Alberta has been requested by Dominion Government to increase beet sugar production -- surveys show widespread labor shortage for farms and especially for hand labor in beets -- while there is widespread community sentiment against oriental movement into our districts, farmers would be willing to use governmental supervised labor apparently available from other districts -- if the Dominion Dept. of Labor organizes controls, assume responsibility for and removes such labor at completion of employment -- groups can be employed under labor contracts at good wages from May until November. District can use one thousand workers and these people should be selected from farm experience with disloyal elements and agitators eliminated."

In this early telegram we see the first public appearance of the items that were eventually to cause a great deal of controversy: first, the degree of supervision, and second, the ultimate removal of labor at the completion of employment. More will be said about these points later, but the seeds of controversy were present before the first Japanese evacuee arrived in Southern Alberta.

On March 6, 1942, the sugar beet growers definitely decided to send a delegation to Vancouver to discuss the situation. There were originally only three members on the delegation -- later increased to four in Vancouver. Mr. Philip Baker represented the Alberta Sugar Beet Growers' Association, Mr. Frank Taylor represented the Canadian Sugar Factories Ltd., and Mr. A.E. Palmer represented the Dominion Department of Agriculture. The City of Lethbridge had refused to send a delegate at first, but once in Vancouver, Alderman J.A. Jardine, who was on vacation there, was persuaded to join the committee. After confirmation from Lethbridge, he was made the official representative of the City of Lethbridge.[18] They met with the newly formed B.C. Security Commission that had been formed on March 4, 1942. The three commissioners: Mr. Austin Taylor, a well-known Vancouver businessman; Mr. F.J. Mead, assistant commissioner of the R.C.M.P.; and Mr. John Shirras, assistant commissioner of the B.C. Provincial Police, were asked to be in attendance at the meeting. The Deputy Secretary of State was also requested to be in attendance at the meeting with the beet growers.

The meeting was a very fortunate one and the various members of the Southern Alberta delegation came away more convinced that the Japanese should come to the sugar beet fields. First, the need was tremendous and no other source of labour seemed in sight. Next, the delegation felt that if the Dominion deemed it necessary to evacuate the Japanese, then it was their duty to help remove them. Thirdly, since the Japanese could be moved to the sugar beets as a family unit, the growers felt that it would be in the interests of the Japanese themselves if they came to Southern Alberta. The police commissioners gave a very favourable report concerning the loyalty of the Japanese, and this insured that a favourable response from the beet growers would be forthcoming. Undoubtedly, the first consideration, that of need, was the most overwhelming one. Nonetheless, the telegram of confirmation addressed to the Honourable Humphrey Mitchell, minister of labour, in care of Austin C. Taylor, on March 16, 1942, gives the following reasoning:[19]

> "Regardless of considerable opposition we believe saner citizens for patriotic reasons would support policy of bringing Japanese families here under strict supervision of Security Commission in accordance with Commissioner's commitments to us if you as Minister of Labour would assure us that both Japanese Canadian Citizens and Japanese aliens would be removed at close of emergency."

"Removed at close of emergency" became an important issue in future negotiations with the Provincial Government of Alberta, and added greatly to the insecurity of the Japanese. As early as March 4, the controversy concerning the bringing in of Japanese was brought up in the Alberta Legislature and Premier Aberhart was questioned about control measures on the Japanese and whether they could come "when and where they like".[20] At this time James Walker, M.L.A. from Warner, asked concerning another future controversy, that of whether or not the Dominion Government would assist in providing a special grant for educating the children of the evacuees.[21] On March 11, 1942, Mr. Walker announced that some 580 Japanese families might be brought into the sugar beet areas of Southern Alberta. In reply, Premier Aberhart said that the provincial government had no power to stop the movement of the Japanese, but that the government did not want to see the Japanese "gathered in Alberta".[22] Provincial opposition continued throughout the war period. Basically the demands of the provincial government were summed in the following resolution reported in the April edition of the Lethbridge Herald:[23]

> "Provincial legislature passed a resolution asking that the Japanese be kept under constant federal supervision to prevent espionage or sabotage, that any costs involved such as health and education should be the responsibility of the Dominion and that

the Japanese be removed from the province at the end of the war."

In Southern Alberta, opposition to the movement of large numbers of Japanese into the area was immediate. Southern Albertans were quite aware of the controversy raging in British Columbia concerning the Japanese question and many were afraid that the problem was simply being exported to Southern Alberta. Many of the popular misconceptions and prejudices common in B.C. were being circulated in the region, and there was a real fear that these 'Japs' might be 'fifth column' workers. The earliest movement of Japanese into the area was probably into Raymond. Many of the 'old timers' among the Japanese had invited their friends and relatives from B.C. By March 11, 1942, some 45 Japanese were registered by the R.C.M.P. in Raymond as having come from B.C.[24] These people came by themselves and were not brought in by the B.C. Security Commission.

This arrival of Japanese from the B.C. coast caused some concern in Raymond, and on March 8, the Canadian Legion called a meeting to discuss the situation. The Herald states that "the Legion from the start has been strongly opposed to the movement of these enemy aliens to the district".[25] Considerable emphasis was made in the articles referring to this movement, that the Japanese leaders gave assurance that these newcomers had been permitted to come by the Canadian authorities. Nevertheless, the protests continued, and on March 11, the Taber branch of the Legion formed a committee to draft a protest concerning the bringing in of Japanese workers. "If the Japanese are needed then they should be under military supervision" was the cry.[26] On March 11, the Lethbridge Board of Trade and a committee from Raymond introduced a bill in the provincial legislature through Solon Low, provincial treasurer, to "prohibit sales of land to any enemy aliens or Hutterites, this bill was intended to stop the acquisition of land by

Japanese and other aliens and to prevent their permanent settling in the area. The bill was passed, but was later disallowed by the federal government.[28] Roy Lee, M.L.A. for Taber, was another individual that was quite vocal concerning the Japanese question and on March 20, stated in the legislature that "he opposed any Japanese coming into the beet fields and taking the place of other workers".[29] This in essence was a repetition of the same arguments made against the Japanese in 1908.

The situation in the City of Lethbridge was somewhat more complicated. Under the agreement made between the city and the B.C. Security Commission, the Japanese brought into the area were to be strictly regulated and were not to be allowed into the city. Article ten of this agreement between the city and the commission reads as follows:[30]

> "The commission further agrees to see that any Japanese so moved remain domiciled on the farms to which they are allocated and the commission further agrees that they will not allow them to move and reside in the City of Lethbridge or become a charge on any municipality in the Provi e of Alberta."

Generally speaking, the members of City Council were opposed to the importation of the Japanese into the area, but allowed it because of 'patriotic reasons' and because of the extreme need of the beet farmers. Alderman Rorie Knight declared "I will have nothing to do with the Japanese -- they are the most treacherous nation on earth. No word of mine will bring a Jap to this country."[31] However, Mayor D.H. Elton stated the opinion of the Council in this manner:[32]

> "We must subdue our personal feelings and cooperate with the government on this problem. There must be unity of sentiment."

It must be noted, however, that not everyone was against the bringing in of Japanese to Southern Alberta. Mayor P.W. Cope of Raymond was particularly unexcited by the impending Japanese immigration. A letter addressed to him and printed in the Raymond Recorder shows some of the feelings held by some individuals in the district concerning the Mormons and the Japanese:[33]

> "Why in the name of God are you allowing the Mormons to bring in all them Japs, all they want to do is to get cheap labor. Why not give some of the poor people the same chance you are giving the Japs. Don't they think of their young people, the life of the cominity (sic) if they bring in all of those Japs...I think a few of those good Mormons who are trying so hard to get something for nothing (of course that is the Mormons anyway) had better go to Japan to live. Raymond has lots of poor people who could do with a little help. They are kicked in the face and Japs are given the chances. Is Japan doing the same by our boys, fighting for them, you and us. No. For God sake Mr. Mayor act before it is too late."

The Mayor's answer was brief and to the point.

> "May I say that the accusations respecting the Mormons and the Japanese coming into Raymond are entirely false and without foundation."

Members of the Lethbridge Northern Beet Growers in the Picture Butte District, also gave unaminous approval for the use of Japanese workers in the sugar beet fields.[34] However, this type of approval seemed limited to the sugar beet growers and to the few individuals in Raymond and Hardieville who were familiar with the Japanese because of their contacts with the old Japanese residents.

Meetings organized by the locals of the Sugar Beet Growers' Association were organized in Raymond and Taber, besides the one held in Picture Butte. In the Taber meeting about half of the growers seemed in favour of bringing in the Japanese while the other half were vehemently opposed.[35] In Raymond, the meeting to discuss the final plans for bringing in the Japanese was hotly debated. Some sixty farmers were present; and although it appeared as if a majority were in favour of the move, there was a vocal minority that was very much opposed.[36]

Despite great controversy and debate concerning the matter, by April it was quite definite that the Japanese would be coming to Southern Alberta. Some forty farmers had applied for more than 45 Japanese families, and on March 31, 1942, fifteen of these sugar beet farmers were prepared to accept the first contingent.[37] Some concern was expressed as to whether the Japanese could purchase or lease land. On March 12, 1942, Austin C. Taylor wrote to the beet growers to reassure them that according to Order-in-Council P.C. 1457, no Japanese was allowed to purchase, lease, rent or acquire land.[38] This did not, however, apply to land held before February 26, 1942, and so did not affect the old residents.[39] With this last item cleared up, the way was open to bring the Japanese into the district.

On April 7, 1942, Mr. W. Andrews of Lethbridge was appointed as the representative of the B.C. Security Commission in Southern Alberta and an office was obtained in the Metcalfe building. Approximately one week later, the first contingent of Japanese evacuees arrived and went to the Coalhurst-Diamond City region. They were from the Mission area of B.C. The second group consisting of 22 families totalling 124 persons arrived from Whonnack, B.C. and took up residence in Picture Butte. The third group of some 73 persons in ten families from Steveston arrived the next day and went to Coaldale. The fourth group comprised of 23 families from New Westminster was bound for the Raymond-Magrath district. The twenty-first group arrived in the first week of June, bringing the total number of Japanese brought into Southern Alberta from B.C. to approximately 2,250 or about 370 families.[40]

Most of these first contingents of Japanese were from the Fraser Valley and had some farm experience. However, later groups included large numbers of fishermen and individuals with lumbering experience. As a result, a great many problems in adjusting were experienced. Dr. La Violette listed four major problems immediately encountered by the evacuees. They were: 1. inadequate living quarters; 2. lack of adequate water supply; 3. the vast spaces between farms and neighbours, and the inadequate medical facilities; 4. lack of acreage and extra work to allow most Japanese families to make an adequate living.[41]

Previous sugar beet labourers had been of the transient nature and so most living quarters were of a temporary sort, adequate for the summer but terribly lacking for winter. As a consequence, the commission was forced to provide lumber in order to rennovate some of the buildings and in some cases even to build homes to accommodate the Japanese. The lack of adequate water was a source of irritation for the Japanese. Water often had to be brought by truck from long distances and adequate cisterns with filters were not ready. The Japanese used a great deal more water than the other workers had, and the farmers were not used to this type of situation:[42]

> "One farmer wrote to the Lethbridge office of the Commission, saying that the Hungarians used only five gallons of water per day while the Japanese used sixty. He asked if it was his responsibility to supply as much water as this because he had no water wagon with which to haul it eight miles."

The vast spaces in Southern Alberta between farms caused a great deal of anxiety among the Japanese and they were constantly afraid of becoming sick and being unable to get medical attention. Medical expenses were high and as a result, the commission was often forced to pay the costs. Originally, movement to the sugar beet fields was meant to allow the Japanese to be self-sufficient. Because of inexperience for the type of work expected of them and the lack of sufficient workers in some families, many were not able to make enough money to sustain them through the first winter. Sugar beet work requires a great deal of hand labour; if only two people out of a family of five is able to work, it is impossible to make an adequate living.

As a result, the commission had to provide relief funds. An estimated 42% of the Japanese were on some type of relief during the first winter.[43] Certain maladjustments were bound to occur, but generally speaking the Japanese proved to be excellent workers. Numerous reports to the Lethbridge Herald during this period lauded the Japanese workers. The following comment by sugar factory officials is typical:[44]

> "...reports from the Canadian Sugar Factory agricultural officials are that most of the Japanese are adapting themselves quite well to their new task of beet thinning. Moreover, the male workers are being assisted in the beet fields by their wives and children, who seemingly enjoy, so far, working in the beets."

The 1942 crop was extremely bountiful and the future looked bright for the Japanese. However, many serious problems lay ahead, and it was not long before they began to surface.

2. Controversy

The controversy concerning the decision to bring the Japanese into Southern Alberta continued to rage. In many ways it never really abated; it was only that as the war progressed towards its end, fewer people paid attention to it. One cannot be overly critical of some of the statements made by individuals during the war years. A type of hysteria did sweep the district when the allied reverses were at their worst, and this unreasonable fear never did really leave. Complaints and problems concerning the Japanese were generally centered around three main issues. They were as follows: 1. funding of added educational costs for Japanese evacuee children; 2. the adequate supervision of Japanese in the cities and towns of the region; 3. the ultimate removal of the evacuated Japanese from Alberta at the conclusion of the war. There were always, of course, the complaints based on racism; although they decreased in intensity near the end of the war, they never did end. A typical example of the racial argument was that made by the Taber Legion in 1942:[45]

> "Resolved that the Taber Branch of the Canadian Legion goes on record as absolutely opposing children of Japanese origin mingling or associating under any pretense whatever with our children."

This was not an isolated incident as many individuals expressed the fear that the importation of a large number of Orientals into the area would lead to the intermingling of the two races, which would ultimately have dire results for the white race.

The first problem concerning school facilities was much debated by various school boards and also in the provincial legislature.[46] The B.C. Security Commission paid an outright grant to the provincial government, which in turn distributed it to the school districts for the education of Japanese children throughout the first eight grades. This grant was $65 per pupil and was the highest in the Dominion. Despite the controversy, the initial numbers of Japanese children that accompanied their parents were not as large as expected, as many of the school-age children remained in the interior housing projects in order to complete their school year.[47] However, as time passed and more of the children accompanied their parents, additional school rooms were built and some extra teachers were hired. The federal government agreed to pay only up to grade eight, and students wishing to go on to high school had to pay their own fees. This sometimes cost as much as $70 per child every year. The Japanese resisted this imposition bitterly, and while the amount varied in different districts, some districts never did require this fee. The children encountered few difficulties in the various schools. Occasionally an incident arose where the white children would call the Japanese children 'Japs' and a fight and crying session would arise. However, no wholesale attempt to discriminate or segregate the Japanese children was made.[48] Although Ottawa still complained about the high costs of education in Alberta, by 1944 the school question had ended.

The second problem concerning the adequate supervision of Japanese was a little more complicated. Generally, this involved two aspects; 1. the problem as seen from the urban areas, more particularly the City of Lethbridge, and 2. the problem as seen by the rural residents. The Lethbridge city council was very anxious to enforce article #10 of the agreement made between the B.C. Security Commission and the City of Lethbridge when the Japanese were first brought into Southern Alberta. According to this section, the Commission was not to "allow them (Japanese) to move and reside in the city of Lethbridge". The Japanese could shop in Lethbridge during the day, but could not live or work in the city. Four very interesting cases developed that challenged this resolution by the city and the commission.

The first incident might be termed the 'beer parlor case'. It illustrates to what extent some of the regulations concerning the Japanese went. On July 27, the Herald reported that the Union of Alberta Municipalities had passed a resolution stating that Japanese should be barred from Alberta beer parlors. This motion had been made by Alderman E.H. Star of Calgary and Mayor D.H. Elton of Lethbridge.[49] Subsequently, city council debated the reasoning behind the move. Mayor Elton explained that he feared that it was not a condition conducive for harmony when servicemen drank beer at one table and saw a group of Japanese at another. Alderman Jardine objected to the singling out of just the Japanese, and in the course of the discussion Germans and Italians were also mentioned as possible being excluded. Further action was not taken until August 4, 1942, when Alderman

J.A. Jardine introduced a motion resolving:[50]

> "That the Alberta Liquor Control Board be and is hereby requested to order all beer parlors in the City of Lethbridge to prohibit the entrance thereto of all Japanese and Hutterites."

Mayor Elton stated that "keeping these people out of beer parlors is a measure for their own protection". No complaints or disturbances had occurred at any time duringgthis period. The possible trouble existed in the councillor's minds. On September 1, 1942, the resolution appeared effectively squashed when J.A. King, chairman of the Alberta Liquor Control Board, informed council that:[51]

> "I have to advise you that our legal department offers the opinion that the board has no authority to undertake to deprive groups of any nationality from patronizing beer parlors in the province of Alberta."

Nonetheless, no doubt motivated somewhat by the controversy on the subject and anxious to avoid all semblance of trouble, the B.C. Security Commission ruled that Japanese "of all citizenship status or otherwise" be prohibited as of January 1, 1943 from frequenting beer parlors".[52] On February 5, 1943, the Commission itself was dissolved; as a result on March 5, 1943, the comedy finally ended. On this date the province rescinded the order forbidding the Japanese from frequenting Alberta beer parlors.[53]

The second case might be termed the 'canning commotion'. On August 11, 1942, a headline in the local newsppaer read "Japanese in Lethbridge are sent back to their farms".[54] Apparently some 42 Japanese had moved into within the city limits, 20 of them to work at the Broder Canning Factory. Advised of this breech of the agreement between the Security Commission and the city, W. A. Eastwood, general manager of the commission, wired the city asking:[55]

> "Does the action of Broder Canning factory Lethbridge in employing Japanese within city limits meet with approval of

Lethbridge city council? We must have approval of council before
Japanese can remain in the city."

The answer was 'no' and in accordance with the agreement action began to
return the Japanese to the farms they had originally been allocated to.
However, on the next day E.J. Gordon, assistant foods administer in Ottawa,
requested that the Japanese be allowed to remain because of the lack of
labour capable of assisting at the canning factory. Mayor D.H. Elton cabled
the following reply:[56]

> "If no other labour is available council will acquiece in your
> request to permit Japanese labour to remain here from the next 7 to
> 10 days. This permission is strictly conditioned upon removal
> within the time specified in your telegram and also on the enforce-
> ment of the agreement entered into with the B.C. Security Commission."

In obedience to this resolution, On August 21, some ten days after the
original request J.N. Lister of the Security Commission announced that the
Japanese were being returned to their farms on that day.[57] On September 1,
1942, it was noted that some 25 Japanese were still being employed by Broder
Canning and the Council expressed their disapproval.[58] Sensing defeat of
their intentions, City Council finally approved the use of Japanese labour
and on January of 1943 resolved:[59]

> 1. "That this Council consents to the hiring of male Japanese
> evacuees from the Province of B.C. by the Broder Canning Company.
>
> 2. That -- housing of Japanese so hired shall be at a Dormitory
> at the plant of the said Broder Canning Company or as closely
> contiguous there to as possible.
>
> 3. That each hiring shall only be for the months of July, August
> and September and Japanese hired as aforesaid shall return to
> their domicile outside the city upon termination of such employ-
> ment."

On June 6, 1944, when all semblance of observing the resolution seemed
doomed, Council granted Broder Canning permission to employ Japanese until
the end of the year.[60]

Taber also was embroiled in a similar commotion when on August 25, 1942, it was announced that Japanese were working in the canning factory there.[61] The Taber branch of the Canadian Legion sent a protest to the B.C. Security Commission stating that they had been assured that the Japanese would only be hired on farms.[62] Nothing more was heard about the issue in 1945. So ended the 'canning commotion'.

The third item dealt with two individual cases - that of a single high school student and of a chick sexer. On October 14, 1942, the city council agreed to allow a certain Japanese youth to take up residence in the city to pursue his high school education. Aldermen Ed Castles and Fred Smeed opposed the action, but in granting the permission council did so with the following stipulation:[63]

> "That the youth alone be permitted to take up residence for schooling purposes. When he finished his schooling he must return to the farm to which his family was allocated. The family cannot take up residence here."

A.E. Russell, the B.C. Security Commission representative, had to appear personally on behalf of the boy, and was reminded that this action was not to be taken as a precedence. But no similar problems came up, even though 15 or so Japanese students eventually did attend high schools in Lethbridge. The most interesting case, however, is that of a certain Japanese chick sexer. Apparently, a poultry firm desperately required his assistance. So on February 1, 1944, after considerable controversy the Japanese chick sexer from Taylor Lake Siding, B.C. was allowed to remain in the city with the provision that he was to be "returned to the neighbouring province by July 1."[64]

Perhaps the most long lasting controversy stemmed around the employment of Japanese domestics in the city, and we will entitle this the "Japanese maid caper". In August of 1943, the St. Michael's Hospital requested permission to employ Japanese domestics to assist in work within the hospital. The question was eventually tabled and the matter left.[65] Later, permission was denied. In February of 1944, after the affair concerning the chick sexer, a Charles O. Asplund wrote a letter to the editor pointing the following out:

> "I should like to ask the city council if it is not being a little naive in spending time discussing special permission to let a single Japanese individual domicile in the city? This question is asked in the light of the fact that there are now and have been for some time several Japanese domestics working in the city."

In essence, the matter remained dormant until April of 1945 when in the face of repeated violations of the agreement, City Council asked the various local organizations in the city of Lethbridge whether they supported Council on its stand concerning observance of the B.C. Security Commission agreement. The Trades and Labour Council strongly endorsed the city's stand, stating in a resolution:[67]

> "That this council will not countenance any Japanese evacuees being employed or domiciled in the City of Lethbridge unless they have first made application to the city council and if application is granted that they must have the necessary permits from the B.C. Security Commission and the R.C.M.P."

Soon after, in a joint statement, the Canadian Legion and the Army and Navy Veterans League urged City Council to "keep out the Japs."[68] Reaction to the stand taken by the Council was immediate. Some members pointed out some of the inconsistencies in their own stand. Acting Mayor T.E. Brown pointed out that: "Many of the Japanese are Canadian born and who are we to deprive them of privileges given to Germans."[69] A letter to the editor stated that if Council was really serious about their stand, why didn't they pass a by-law and enforce it. The writer went on to state:[70]

> "Now it is proposed that anyone wishing to employ a Japanese maid should apply to the city council. Since when has it been the business of the city council to decide whether or not a person should have a maid and if so, whether or not she should be Japanese?"

Similarly, in a letter to the Herald the executive of the Presbyterial of the Women's Missionary Society of the United Church in Southern Alberta pointed out that:[71]

> "The outcry against the Japanese girls who are honestly desiring to earn an independent livelihood in our city is the sort of racial discrimination adopted by the Nazis."

Despite being called Nazis and racists, the Lethbridge City Council remained firm. War with Japan ended in August of 1945, but on October 10, 1945, another request by St. Michael's Hospital to employ Japanese domestics was turned down.[72] The B.C. Security Commission had been dissolved by Order-in-Council P.C. 946 on February 5, 1943, but it was found that the agreement with the Commission was still in effect and being administered by the Department of Labour. Despite its firmness, the hopeless position of the City Council was pointed out by Alderman Edward Castles who said: "that since the department of labour took them (the Japanese) over, lots of them have come into the city. The war is over and no one seems to care."[73] This seemed a fitting epitaph to the controversy aroused by the hiring of Japanese domestics some two years before.

The farmers in the area wanted more stringent supervision of the Japanese workers mostly because they were afraid that the Japanese would move away to other more lucrative jobs. As long as they were confined to the farms to which they had been allocated, the beet farmers were assured of a permanent source of labour. At the 1944 Annual Meeting of the Beet Growers' Association, President Phil Baker stated:[74]

> "With respect to Japanese labour it must be emphasized that the free movement of Japanese workers and the members of their families within this area has imposed a hardship on producers."

Many Japanese families found that they were unable to make sufficient money working solely on the farms to which they had been allocated. As a result,

any moved and changed locations attracted by larger acreages and better
conditions. This angered some farmers who felt that the Japanese were somewhat in the nature of 'slave' labour and should remain on the farms to which
they were assigned. Many farmers had gone to considerable expense to
improve living quarters and they were incensed when the Japanese families
moved on to better areas. As the war progressed, the labour situation became
even more acute, and very few Japanese families followed the first contingents.
In July of 1943, Humphrey Mitchell, minister of labour, stated that:[75]

> "They (the Japanese) saved the sugar beet industry: but I do not see any chance of Southern Alberta getting any more."

In the light of rapidly decreasing labour supplies, the farmers were anxious
to keep the Japanese 'domiciled on the farms to which they were allocated'
but easing restrictions frustrated this attempt and very little could be done
about it.

The next great controversy centered around the demand by the Province of
Alberta that the Japanese be removed from Alberta at the end of the hostilities. The whole concept was that the relocation of the Japanese in Southern
Alberta was only a temporary measure and that at the conclusion of the war
the Japanese would again be returned to B.C. Apparently, contained in the
agreement signed between the provinces and the federal government was the
stipulation that the government would remove the Japanese upon request, six
months after hostilities ceased.[76] The political situation was such that,
although the Social Credit Party appeared firmly entrenced in Alberta, they
could not afford to antagonize various segments of the province on the
Japanese question. A number of groups concurred with the provincial
government's demand that the federal government live up to its commitments.
At the 1944 annual meeting, Phil Baker of the Beet Growers' Association

reiterated their position:[77]

> "I wish to go on record that, when the emergency under which the Japanese now in this district were brought in, has ceased, all Japanese personnel here must be returned to the places from whence they came."

It is doubtful that the farmers really expected to see this occur, but the clause was there just the same and caused great anxiety among the Japanese. At meetings of the Union of Alberta Municipalities both in 1942 and also in 1944, a resolution was passed which in essence stated that they were opposed to the permanent establishment of the Japanese in Alberta and that at the conclusions of hostilities the Japanese be removed "in order that our men and women serving in the armed forces will be found room to re-establish themselves in occupations desirable to them."[78] Since all those advocating removal were quite aware of the opposition in B.C. to the re-establishment of Japanese in that province, one wonders where the federal government was expected to send the Japanese. It is not unlikely that there was a large minority in Alberta who advocated repatriation to Japan as a possible solution. Opposition to the stand of the provincial government did come from a variety of areas, but the strongest stand came from the United Church at a conference held in Calgary in 1945:[79]

> "Canada's handling of Japanese Canadians has been a blot on our record as a people...We strongly disapprove of Premier Manning's declaration that in any resettlement of B.C. Japanese throughout the dominion, Alberta would refuse the quote assigned to this province."

They also came out against repatriation to Japan. Like many other controversies a firm decision on this matter was avoided, and the whole matter was allowed to lapse until the federal government allowed the contract to expire on March 31, 1948. Throughout this entire period the Japanese were never sure when they would be requested to leave, and the resulting anxiety is impossible to assess.

The previous discussion would make it appear as if Lethbridge was the only area in which considerable controversy had occurred. This was not so. On April 7, 1942, the Medicine Hat city council declined to approve a request from King Hirano, Japanese resident of the city for over 20 years, to permit his brother and family from Vancouver to come to Medicine Hat for the duration:[80]

> "The council decided it could not assist in any way in bringing Japanese into this area and reaffirmed its stand taken in a resolution a fortnight ago that all Japanese should be kept to ther under government supervision rather than be distributed across the Dominion piecemeal."

In Calgary, Hiroshi Kuwahara was refused permission to return to the city where he had grown up as a boy. He had been working in Vancouver when the evacuation order came, so he requested permission to return to Calgary, where his family resided and owned a store. In a hotly debated council meeting, his request was denied. Nonetheless, the B.C. Security Commission allowed him to quietly slip into Calgary without permission, and nothing more was heard about the issue.[81] Edmonton similarly made restrictions against the Japanese. An example occurred in September of 1945, nearly a month after the cessation of hostilities between the allies and Japan. K. Kenneth Isaoka of Iron Springs requested permission to reside in Edmonton while attending university, but the city fathers ruled that no Japanese student would be allowed to come to the city "until all applications by servicemen have been filled".[82]

The Japanese evacuees sometimes prompted the controversy themselves. In Raymond the Buddhist Church decided to have activities such as Judo and Kendo in order to provide wholesome activity for their young people. This resulted in several rumours being circulated in the Town of Raymond that the

Japanese were training their young people in various martial arts, preparatory for 'fifth column' work in the area. Some concern was expressed by members of the community, and as a result, a group of prominent citizens were asked to attend some of these 'so-called' subversive activities. This group included the mayor, bankers, and school principals. Apparently satisfied by what they had seen, the controversy ended.[83] This pointed out how vital it was for the existence of responsible Japanese leaders who could communicate with both the Japanese and Caucasian residents. It was in this role that the 'old-timers' among the Japanese in Raymond proved particularly invaluable.

The B.C. Security Commission also recognized the necessity of having people close at hand who were aware of the problems and difficulties. Mr. William Andrews was made their appointee in Lethbridge on April 7, 1942. He was replaced on August 31, 1942 by A.E. Russell. These individuals played a very vital role in smoothing over the resulting difficulties between the Japanese and the growers and between the growers and the Security Commission. During 1943, a problem arose in that the beet growers desired a great many more Japanese workers, but the Japanese in the interior camps were reluctant to come. Apparently various rumours concerning the poor housing, lack of water and the inability of certain families to earn a living were circulating throughout the camps. The harsh climate of Alberta was another reason which discouraged the evacuees from coming to Southern Alberta. In this instance, the Security Commission had Mr. T. Maruno appointed as a Japanese spokesman, and he travelled with Mr. A.E. Russell through the relocation camps in order to persuade more families to come, attempting to discredit some of the rumours.[84] It is doubtful that he was able to allay many of the fears, but from this time on increasing use is made of Japanese spokesmen in negotiations with the beet growers and the Japanese workers. The opinions of the Japanese were slowly being considered.

Acceptance did not come quickly, and public opinion in favour of the Japanese took a long time to develop.

3. Acceptance

It is difficult to assess exactly when the Japanese began to be accepted as potential permanent residents in Southern Alberta. Perhaps they never were really accepted until long after the war had ended. Nonetheless, this acceptance did occur and one important indication of this was when the newspapers ceased to headline articles about the 'Japs'. It is interesting to note that during the very first part of the Pacific war, the Lethbridge Herald would headline articles concerning the Japanese in Japan and the Japanese in Southern Alberta with the term 'Japs'. By 1943, an interesting differentiation had occurred and the Japanese Canadians were usually referred to as the 'Japanese', a much less derogatory term, while the Japanese in Japan were still being called 'Japs'. Although not especially a champion of Japanese rights, the Lethbridge Herald did advocate moderation and attempted to lend reason to an obviously irrational situation. As early as July, 1942, the Herald in an editorial entitled "The Japanese Among Us" cautioned that:[85]

"The possibility however, that an apparently well-disposed Japanese working far inland on an Alberta farm, could become a source of danger of any sort is exceedingly remote."

The apparent concern of the United Church women and also the United Church as a whole indicated growing awareness of the injustices in the treatment of the Japanese in Canada. Albertans were not immune to prejudices, but neither were they immune to the groundswell of opposition to the government's stand on the Japanese as the war with Japan neared to its close.

As the Japanese became more and more a part of the local scene, individuals began to ignore discriminatory regulations. In the fall of 1943, some 250 Japanese were allowed to go to work in various saw mills and lumber camps in Alberta. Some worked in Macleod, Burmis, Rocky Mountain House, and the Lesser Slave Lake region. They returned in the spring of 1944, demonstrating their trustworthiness.[86] Although during 1943, the Japanese evacuees had a special method prescribed to them in order to get their ration books, by the following year, the Japanese were asked to pick up their ration books at local distribution centres in the city of Lethbridge and throughout the district, in the same manner as other residents.[87] The same was true of other restrictions. At first, the R.C.M.P. were very diligent in checking on the evacuees, but later became increasingly lax in enforcing the various resolutionssof the Security Commission. The just and humane handling of the situation by R.C.M.P. officers did much to alleviate an otherwise intolerable situation, and they did much to gain the respect of the Japanese.

Local residents appeared surprised that the Japanese could speak English and that many of them were Canadian born. An article carried in the Herald reflects this amazement:[88]

> "Japanese beet workers, many of them speaking perfect English, are in the Taber district and are seen frequently on the t n streets. Some of them have been members of Christian churches at the coast and attend Sunday services here."

Obviously, if the people in Southern Alberta had been better informed such an item would never have made news. Of all the towns in Southern Alberta, Raymond was able to accept the Japanese most easily. Most of this can be ascribed to the fact that some 300 Japanese had resided in the district for more than 30 years. This in itself was a testimony to the white residents that all Japanese were not necessarily disloyal, and it proved to the evacuees that it was possible for Japanese to get along quite well with the white residents in Southern Alberta.

It might also be noted here that several quite prominent individuals came to visit with the Japanese evacuees in Southern Alberta during the course of the war. In July of 1942, Pedro Edward Shwartz, Spanish Consul-General in Canada, visited the Lethbridge district. Spain had been appointed as the High Protecting Power for Japanese interests in Canada. In conversation with the Lethbridge Herald the consul-general refused to say that everything was satisfactory concerning the Japanese in the district.[89]

> "Things are gradually being worked out but it will require a good deal of adjustment. To say satisfactory would indicate that everything has been worked out smoothly. This is not the case as yet."

Accompanying Mr. Schwartz were Commissioner J.P. Mead of the R.C.M.P., and Alfred Rive representing the Canadian Government. Mr. Andrews, Philip Baker, H. G. Houlton, and M. Cudo acting as an interpreter for the consul-general, accompanied the party in Southern Alberta. It is doubtful that the consul-general had much to do with solving any of the numerous problems encountered by the Japanese in Southern Alberta, but as we can see from the quote above, he did serve a function by pointing out some of the problems and injustices that existed. He did demonstrate that someone was interested in the welfare of the evacuees, and that someone would be checking periodically to hear complaints from the Japanese evacuees. In January of 1943 a representative of the International Red Cross also visited the district and inspected living and working conditions.[90] The reason these visits were so important and such great pains were taken to create a favourable impression was that some 2000 Canadian soldiers, some of them from Southern Alberta, were being held prisoner by the Japanese after the Hong Kong fiasco. The Canadian Government was anxious that no action on their part in treating the Japanese in Canada would give excuse to the Japanese to further abuse those

Canadians they had in their custody in Japan and China. Many Canadian Japanese were being held in various internment camps and road camps in Canada. One of these camps was near Seebe, Alberta not far from Banff.[91] These men were Japanese nationals, and the treatment given to them might determine the treatment meted to Canadian nationals held in Japanese territory.

In June of 1944, Dr. Forrest E. La Violette, visited Lethbridge and made the following comment, which no doubt made many Southern Albertans think a little more deeply about their treatment of the Japanese in Canada:[92]

> "It is the belief of the research worker, Canadians will be judged in the post-war period according to the manner in which they behave toward their own Japanese nationals."

One should not be unduly harsh upon the residents of Southern Alberta during this emotional period. Rumours of Japanese infiltrators, and other vindictive gossip directed against the Japanese was very common. Every newspaper edition carried yet another example of 'Jap brutality'. In 1945, some Japanese balloons were discovered in the area. Apparently they carried some incendiary bombs and might have started forrest fires and other damage had they worked. Southern Albertans were naturally concerned about this 'invasion' of Canadian territory. Therefore, one can understand to some extent why Southern Albertans were slow to accept the Japanese Canadians during World War II.

FOOTNOTES

1. Lethbridge Herald. Dec. 8, 1941.
2. None of the local residents recall this registration.
3. As far as we know, no Japanese from Southern Alberta was interned.
4. Lethbridge Herald. Dec. 8, 1941.
5. Lethbridge Herald. Dec. 13, 1941.
6. ibid. Dec. 13, 1941.
7. ibid. Dec. 8, 1941.
8. Interview with Mr. H. Kuwahara.
9. Interview with Mr. H. Kuwahara.
10. Lethbridge Herald. Jan. 2, 1942.
11. Alberta Sugar Beet Growers' Association Papers. op.cit.
12. ibid.
13. ibid.
14. Kimiaki Nakashima. Economic Aspects of the Japanese Evacuation from the Canadian Pacific Coast. op.cit., p. 19.
15. See the Lethbridge Herald. Feb. 20, 1942, the editorial "Japanese Labour".
16. Interview with A.E. Palmer.
17. Alberta Sugar Beet Growers' Association Papers. op.cit.
18. Interview with A.E. Palmer. See also the Lethbridge Herald, Mar. 13, 1942.
19. Alberta Sugar Beet Growers' Association Papers. op.cit.
20. Lethbridge Herald. Mar. 4, 1942.
21. ibid. Mar. 4, 1942.
22. ibid. Mar. 11, 1942.
23. ibid. Apr. 1, 1942.
24. ibid. Mar. 11, 1942.
25. ibid. Mar. 9, 1942.
26. ibid. Mar. 11, 1942

27. Lethbridge Herald. Mar. 11, 1942.

28. See Forrest E. Laviolette. The Canadian Japanese and World War II. op.cit., p. 122 - 125.

29. Lethbridge Herald. Mar. 20, 1942.

30. ibid. Mar. 13, 1942. See the appendix #1.

31. ibid. Mar. 11, 1942.

32. ibid. Mar. 11, 1942.

33. Raymond Recorder. Mar. 13, 1942.

34. Lethbridge Herald. Mar. 18, 1942.

35. Interview with A.E. Palmer.

36. Interview with C.D. Peterson. Raymond Recorder. Apr. 3, 1942.

37. Alberta Sugar Beet Growers' Association Papers.

38. Alberta Sugar Beet Growers' Association. Eighteenth Annual Report. Raymond, 1942, p. 26 - 27.

39. Lethbridge Herald. Mar. 5, 1942.

40. Lethbridge Herald. May 30, 1942.

41. Forrest E. Laviolette. The Canadian Japanese and World War II. op.cit., p. 127 - 129.

42. ibid., p. 128.

43. Lethbridge Herald. Jan. 6, 1968.

44. ibid. June 2, 1942.

45. ibid. April 29, 1942.

46. ibid. May 7, 1942 and June 20, 1942.

47. ibid. June 17, 1942.

48. An incident occurred in Raymond where it was suggested that the Buddhist Church be used to hold classes for the Japanese children brought into the area during the evacuation. It was feared that this might lead to segregated classes, and so the Japanese opposed this and the idea was quickly dropped.

49. Lethbridge Herald. June 27, 1942.

50. <u>ibid</u>. Aug. 4, 1942. Hutterites were avowed pacifists and they were allowed 'conscientious objectors' status. Since they were of German ancestry and lived in colonies, they were often the object of persecution.

51. <u>ibid</u>. Sept. 1, 1942.

52. <u>ibid</u>. Dec. 7, 1942.

53. <u>ibid</u>. Mar. 5, 1943.

54. <u>ibid</u>. Aug. 11, 1942.

55. <u>ibid</u>. Aug. 11, 1942.

56. <u>ibid</u>. Aug. 12, 1942.

57. <u>ibid</u>. Aug. 21, 1942.

58. <u>ibid</u>. Sept. 1, 1942.

59. <u>ibid</u>. Jan. 13, 1943.

60. <u>ibid</u>. June 6, 1944.

61. <u>ibid</u>. Aug. 25, 1942.

62. <u>ibid</u>. Sept. 1, 1942.

63. <u>ibid</u>. Oct. 14, 1942.

64. <u>ibid</u>. Feb. 1, 1944. Also an interview with Kyoto Shigehiro.

65. <u>ibid</u>. Oct. 8, 1943.

66. <u>ibid</u>. Feb. 5, 1944.

67. <u>ibid</u>. Apr. 6, 1945.

68. <u>ibid</u>. Apr. 10, 1945.

69. <u>ibid</u>. Apr. 10, 1945.

70. <u>ibid</u>. Apr. 13, 1945.

71. <u>ibid</u>. Apr. 21, 1945.

72. <u>ibid</u>. Oct. 10, 1945.

73. <u>ibid</u>. Sept. 25, 1945.

74. <u>ibid</u>. Mar. 2, 1944.

75. <u>ibid</u>. July 15, 1943.

76. ibid. May 6, 1944. See also Forrest E. LaViolette. *The Canadian Japanese and World War II*. op.cit., p. 133 - 4.

77. *Lethbridge Herald*. Mar. 2, 1944.

78. ibid. June 20, 1944.

79. ibid. May 24, 1945.

80. ibid. Apr. 7, 1942.

81. Interview with Hiroshi Kuwahara.

82. *Lethbridge Herald*. Sept. 11, 1945.

83. Interview with Masso Matsugi.

84. *Lethbridge Herald*. Mar. 9, 1943.

85. ibid. July 22, 1942.

86. ibid. Apr. 4, 1944.

87. ibid. Feb. 16, 1943.

88. ibid. Aug. 25, 1942.

89. ibid. July 21, 1942.

90. ibid. Jan. 20, 1943.

91. Chiyokitchi Ariga, and Nabue Ariga. *Omoide no Katami*. Tokyo, 1966.

92. *Lethbridge Herald*. June 29, 1944.

CHAPTER V   The Foundation of a Future

The war in the Pacific ended in August of 1945, but the future of the Japanese in Southern Alberta was not resolved until some time later. It was not until the 1948 Alberta Provincial Election that the evacuated Japanese in Southern Alberta were allowed to exercise their newly won franchise. It was not until April 1, 1949, when the last of the 'Emergency War Measures Acts' were rescinded and full political recognition was given to Japanese Canadians throughout Canada, that the Japanese in Canada were 'truly free'.[1]

A foundation for a future had been laid by the Japanese in Southern Alberta in the some forty years that the Japanese had resided in the area. Southern Albertans had accepted the Japanese as good reliable workers, and undoubtedly, the Japanese had saved the Southern Alberta sugar industry. During the Second World War, they received payment in accordance to regular contracts, and it is estimated that the Japanese in Alberta alone provided at least $750,000 worth of necessary labour."[2] Despite the persecution leveled against them during the war, the Japanese had not allowed themselves to become a burden on the war effort.

Unknowingly, the Japanese who had resided in Alberta prior to 1941 also played a major role in preparing for the future. Although little study has been done in determining how great a factor the presence of Japanese in Southern Alberta since 1905 had in influencing the evacuees, it is quite obvious that because of their efforts, a great deal of the potential hostility directed against the evacuees was placated. Because of their success in adapting to the region and in becoming a part of their communities, the evacuated Japanese were encouraged to remain in the area. No doubt, the example set by the 'old-timers' in the region prior to the war prompted the

Sugar Beet Growers' Association to pursue the task of importing the Japanese evacuees into the area. This argument is confirmed when one realizes that both Philip Baker, then president of the Alberta Sugar Beet Growers' Association, and James H. Walker, M.L.A. had Japanese neighbours, and that throughout the war years they were on amiable relations.

In pursuing the argument that perhaps the Japanese that resided in Southern Alberta prior to the Second World War were an important factor in the eventual acceptance of the evacuated Japanese, we must first determine to what degree the 'old-timers' had become integrated into their communities. Two important indicators of the degree of cultural integration, are the religious affiliations of the individuals involved and the degree with which they have acquired the language of their respective communities. In doing so, let us examine the following tables.[3]

Relgious Affiliations of Japanese in Alberta, 1931

Sex	Christian	Buddhist	Other
Male	247	158	12
Female	138	93	4
TOTAL	385	251	16

Nearly 60% of the Japanese in Alberta claimed Christianity as their religion in 1931. This becomes even more important when one realizes that no Japanese mission existed in Alberta prior to 1942. In fact the only Japanese ministers in Alberta prior to the war were those of the Raymond Buddhist Church. During the war, the only Japanese ministers in the area were Reverend Shinjo Ikuta of the Raymond Buddhist Church and Reverend G.G. Nakayama of the Anglican Church who came to Coaldale during the evacuation. Reverend Yutetsu Kawamura of the Buddhist Church and Reverend Jun Kabayama of the United Church came as sugar beet workers to the area and were officially not classed as ministers of religion.[4] Therefore, although only one indication of growing acculturation by the Japanese, the small numbers of Japanese ministers before World War II meant that a large proportion of the Japanese in Alberta were achieving greater contacts with other nationalities through the church.

The following table reveals that the Japanese in Alberta were also more capable of communicating with their English-speaking neighbours thatn their B.C. counterparts. This would seem to indicate that there were fewer opportunities for misunderstanding and prejudices to develop in Southern Alberta.

Language Ability of All Japanese 10 Years of Age or Over, 1931

Province	Total	% Unable to Speak English	% Male	% Female
Alberta	429	11.89%	6.10%	24.63%
B.C.	15,732	22.04%	15.62%	32.58%

Nearly twice as many Japanese in Alberta in 1931 were able to communicate in English than those in British Columbia. This is a strong indicator of the degree of integration achieved by the Japanese in Alberta.

It is also interesting to note that there were only some 170 aliens of Japanese race in Alberta out of a population of 652 in 1931. In 1931, out of the some 353 persons of Japanese race who had been born in Japan, nearly 70% of them were naturalized Canadian citizens. Since the Japanese population decreased a little during the 1930's, it can be assumed that many of the aliens returned to Japan or to B.C. and that the percentage of those naturalized or Canadian citizens increased by 1941.

On August 4, 1944, Prime Minsiter W.L. Mackenzie King outlined in the House of Commons the government's policy in respect to people of Japanese race in Canada. Basically, the salient features were as follows:[5]

1. "To avoid undue concentration with consequent racial hostility and strife, people of Japanese origin should be distributed more evenly throughout Canada;

2. Those found disloyal to Canada during the war should not have the privilege of remaining in this country, and those desiring to go to Japan voluntarily should be aided and encouraged to do so;

3. Any further Japanese immigration should be prohibited, but without commitments binding indefinitely into the future;

4. People of Japanese origin loyal to Canada should be treated fairly and justly."

In accordance with these general guidelines, on December 17, 1945, three Orders-in-Council were tabled in the House of Commons. Known as the 'deportation orders', Order-in-Council P.C. 7355 listed the following categories of individuals who were ubject to deportation:[6]

1. "Japanese Nationals who had requested repatriation or who remained in internment on September 1, 1945.

2. Naturalized Canadian citizens who requested repatriation and did not revoke their requests in writing before midnight on September 1, 1945.

3. Canadian-born Japanese sixteen years of age or over who requested repatriation, if such persons had not revoked their requests in writing before the issuance of an Order for their deportation.

4. The wife and children (under sixteen years of age) of any person in the above categories for whom the Minister of Labour made an Order for Deportation."

These provisions were strenuously contested, and went as far as the Supreme Court of Canada. Although the validity of many of the orders were in doubt, some 3,964 persons were deported or 'repatriated' before the provisions concerning deportation were revoked in full on January 23, 1947.

Shortly before the war with Japan ended in 1945, the R.C.M.P. completed an inquiry as to how many Japanese in Alberta over the age of sixteen would like to remain in Canada or go to Japan. If they chose to go to Japan, the Dominion Government would pay their fare and turn over any money realized from the sale of their property in B.C. As of August 31, 1945, the results showed that 43.3% of the Japanese in Canada has registered their intention of returning to Japan. This figure included the children under sixteen. In B.C. the percentage was 60.1%, while in Alberta it was only 15.4%. This meant that only 176 of 790 Japanese Nationals and 46 of 432 Naturalized citizens living in Alberta stated their intention to go to Japan. After a series of delays, only nine Japanese from Alberta actually departed for Japan under the 'repatriation' program.[7]

This is probably the strongest testimony to the fact that the Japanese had been well received in Alberta. Although we can only guess as to the reasons for the evacuees wishing to remain in Canada, it is quite probably that the presence of some 578 Japanese in Alberta, many of them since 1905, played an important part in the decision for many evacuees to remain in Canada. By the end of World War II, the Japanese in Southern Alberta were integrating with the communities at a very rapid rate. The Japanese in Southern Alberta had endured many trials and tribulations during the some forty years they had resided in Alberta; and although by 1945 their final status has not yet been resolved, the prosperity and acceptance that had eluded them for so many years seemed finally within their grasp.

FOOTNOTES

1. Program of the 6th Annual Convention of the Alberta Japanese-Canadian Citizen's Association, March 21, 1953.

2. Canada. Dept. of Labour. Report on Administration of Japanese Affairs in Canada, 1942 - 1944. op.cit., p. 37.

3. All information contained in the following two tables has been gleened from the Seventh Census of Canada, 1931. Ottawa, King's Printer. 1934.

4. Refer to Rev. Kabayama's book, Oncho Ki, and Rev. Timothy Nakayama's article, "Anglican Missions to the Japanese in Canada", published in the Journal of the Canadian Church Historical Society.

5. Canada. Dept. of Labour. Report on Re-establishment of Japanese in Canada, 1944 - 46. op.cit., p. 8.

6. ibid. p. 13 - 14. See also p. 11 - 15.

7. Forest E. La Violette. Canadian Japanese and World War II. op.cit., p. 133 and table V. in appendix E.

APPENDIX

App. # 1

INDIVIDUALS INTERVIEWED DURING THE COURSE OF RESEARCH

NAME	YEAR OF ARRIVAL IN SOUTHERN ALBERTA	BIRTHPLACE
Higa, Sucho	1920	Japan, Okinawa
Hironaka, Kaisuke	1918	Japan, Yamaguchi
Hironaka, Dr. Robert	--	Canada, Alberta
Inamasu, Mary	1908	Canada, Alberta
Iwaasa, Ito	1915	Japan, Hiroshima
Iwaasa, Tadao	1910	Japan, Hiroshima
Iwaasa, Toru	1918	Canada, Alberta
Iwaasa, Seiko	1922	Canada, B.C.
Kamitakahara, M.	1908	Japan, Kagoshima
Kanashiro, Taro	1908	Japan, Okinawa
Karaki, Mitsuo	1925	Japan, Nagano
Karaki, Takashi	1909	Japan, Nagano
King, Elizabeth	1903	U.S.A., Utah
Kubota, Takayuki	1917	Japan, Hiroshima
Kuwahara, Mrs. S.	1922	Japan, Shiga
Matsugi, Masao	1917	Japan, Ehime
Oshiro, Mrs. H.	192?	Japan, Okinawa
Palmer, A.E.	1903	U.S.A., Utah
Peterson, Christian	1901	U.S.A., Utah
Peterson, Verne	1903	U.S.A., Utah
Sawada, Mrs. Kahei	1914	Japan, Shiga
Shackleford, A.W.	--	--
Shigehiro, Kyoto	1922	Canada, B.C.
Shima, Kyomasari	1922	Japan, Okinawa
Shimbashi, Zenkitchi	1910	Japan, Kagoshima
Sudo, Hisagi	1908	Japan, Mie
Sugimoto, Kisaburo	1908	Japan, Mie
Takahashi, Joseph	--	Canada, Alberta
Tomiyama, Giichi	1917	Japan, Okayama

App. # 2

AGREEMENT BETWEEN THE B.C. SECURITY COMMISSION AND THE CITY OF LETHBRIDGE AND THE ALBERTA SUGAR BEET GROWERS' ASSOC.*

1. As a war emergency measure, it is essential that all Japanese must be removed from the national defense area restricted to Japanese, to other areas of Canada where they can be taken care of.
2. The Security Commission has full power to control all such movement of Japanese and will assume responsibility for their movement to the district and will move them out of the district as soon as the emergency ceases to exist or they require to be moved in the best interests of the district concerned.
3. The Security Commission will provide supervision at the destination to see that the Japanese are properly placed and housed, in houses provided by the employer.
4. It is understood that such Japanese shall be selected from experienced agricultrual workers and are approved by the R.C.M.P.
5. The Commission will be responsible for keeping strict supervision over Japanese families so moved from the restricted area during the entire period of their domicile in Alberta and if necessary will provide more police protection for the districts in whch they are located.
6. The commission will undertake to make a thorough check on all Japanese who have moved to Southern Alberta. In future, any Japances moved from the restricted area will be on the authority of this commission and by permit from this commission and you can be assured of complete supervision of all Japanese so moved.
7. The responsibility for the education of any or all such Japanese rests with the Security Commission.
8. Families to be moved only at such time in such numbers as required.
9. This commission will guarantee to the city of Lethbridge that no Japanese so moved will become a charge on them for relief, medical services, medicine or hospitalization. Should hospitalization and medical care be required, same will be paid for by the Japanese and, if not, by this commission.
10. The commission further agrees to see that any Japanese so moved remain domiciled on the farm to which they are allocated and the commission further agrees that they will not allow them to move and reside in the city of Lethbridge or become a charge on any municipality in the province of Alberta.
11. It will become an obligation on the employer who employs Japanese help supplied by the commission to pay the regular contract price for labor and provide a garden plot with each house and permit the Japanese to occupy throughout the year a house so provided for him. The Japanese laborer is also to be allowed to improve his house for winter use. It is not expected that the employer will be responsible for the Japanese family or laborer during the period that he is not employed.

Austin C. Taylor, Chairman
B. C. Security Commission

*from the Lethbridge Herald. March 13, 1942

App. #3

BIBLIOGRAPHY OF MATERIAL SPECIFICALLY DEALING WITH THE JAPANESE IN ALBERTA

ARCHIVAL MATERIAL

1. Alberta Sugar Beet Growers' Association Papers. Glenbow-Alberta Institute Library. Calgary, Alberta, Also Annual Reports. Mr. Harry Boyse. Lethbridge, Alta.

2. Canada. Census Reports.

3. Hardieville Doshi Kai. Minute and Roll Book. Mr. Sucho Higa. Hardieville, Alberta.

4. The Lethbridge Herald.

5. Longman, O.S. (research officer). The Beet Sugar Industry in Alberta, Documents. Glenbow-Alberta Institute Library. Calgary, Alberta.

6. Premier's Papers. Provincial Archives. Edmonton, Alberta.

7. The Raymond Recorder. Legislative Library. Edmonton, Alberta.

8. United Mine Workers of America, District #18. Minute Book, Lethbridge Local #574. Glenbow-Alberta Institute Library, Calgary, Alberta.

PRINTED MATERIAL

1. Ariga, Chiyokitchi and Ariga, Nobue. Omoide no Katami. Tokyo, 1966. (in Japanese).

2. Ariga, Chiyokitchi. Rocky no Yuaku. Tokyo, 1951. (in Japanese).

3. Canada. Department of Labour. Report on Administration of Japanese Affairs in Canada, 1942-44. Ottawa, King's Printer, 1945.

4. Canada. Department of Labour. Report on the Re-establishment of Japanese in Canada, 1944-46. Ottawa, King's Printer, 1947.

5. Canadian Japanese Association. The Japanese Contribution to Canada. Vancouver, 1940.

6. Canada Daily News. Canada Nippon-jin Nogyo Hatten Go. Tokyo, Japan, 1930. pages 244-269. (in Japanese).

7. Hicken, J. Orvin (compiler). Raymond Roundup, 1902-1967. Raymond, Alberta, 1967.

8. Kabayama, Rev. Jun. Oncho Ki. Tokyo, Fukuinkan Shoten, 1971. (in Japanese).

9. La Violette, Forrest E. The Canadian Japanese and World War II: A Sociological and Psychological Account. Toronto, U. of T. Press, 1948.

BIBLIOGRAPY (CONT.)

10. Nakashima, Kimiaki. Economic Aspects of the Japanese Evacuation from the Canadian Pacific Coast. Montreal, McGill University M.A. Thesis, 1946.

11. Nakayama, Junshiro. Canada no Hoko. Tokyo, 1921. (in Japanese).

12. Nakayama, Junshiro. Canada Doho Hatten Taikan. Tokyo, 1921. (in Japanese).

13. Nakayama, Timothy M. "Anglican Missions to the Japanese in Canada", Journal of the Canadian Church Historical Society, Vol. 8, No. 2, June 1966, pages 26-45.

14. Nihon Sangyo Kyokai. Dai Jusanji: Sangyo Boeki Korosha Shoseki Ryoku. Tokyo, 1936. page 37. (in Japanese).

15. Palmer, Howard. "Anti-Oriental Sentiment in Alberta 1880-1920", Canadian Ethnic Studies, Vol. 2, No. 2, December 1970, pages 31-58.

16. Palmer, Howard. Land of the Second Chance: A history of ethnic groups in Southern Alberta. Lethbridge, the Lethbridge Herald, 1972.

17. Palmer, Howard. Responses to Foreign Immigration: Nativism and Ethnic Tolerance in Alberta, 1880-1920. Edmonton, University of Alberta M.A. Thesis, 1971.

18. Quo, F.Q. "Ethnic Origin and Political Activities: The Case of Orientals," Canadian Ethnic Studies. Vol. 3, No. 2, December 1971, pages 119-138.

19. Raymond Buddhist Church. A History of Forty Years of the Raymond Buddhist Church. Raymond, 1970. (in Japanese with an English Summary).

20. Sato, Tsutae; Sato, Hanako. Kodomo to Tomo ni Gojunen. Tokyo, 1969. (in Japanese).

21. Tairiku Nippo Sha. Canada Doho Hatten Shi. Vancouver, 1909. (in Japanese).

22. Takami, Hiroto. Canada no Nihonjin. Tokyo, 1969. (in Japanese).

23. Zenkyokai Kyogikai. Canada Nihonjin Godo Kyokai Shi 1892-1959. Toronto, United Church of Canada, 1961. (in Japanese).

THE ASIAN EXPERIENCE IN NORTH AMERICA

An Arno Press Collection

Andracki, Stanislaw. **Immigration of Orientals into Canada with Special Reference to Chinese.** 1979

Bell, Reginald. **Public School Education of Second-Generation Japanese in California.** 1935

California State Board of Control. **California and the Oriental:** Japanese, Chinese, and Hindus. 1922

Canada, Department of Labour. **Two Reports on Japanese Canadians in World War II.** Two vols. in one. 1944/1947

Canada, Royal Commission on Chinese and Japanese Immigration. **Report of the Royal Commission on Chinese and Japanese Immigration.** 1902

Canada, Royal Commission on Chinese Immigration. **Report of the Royal Commission on Chinese Immigration:** Report and Evidence. 1885

Coman, Katharine. **The History of Contract Labor in the Hawaiian Islands.** 1903 *and* Andrew W[illiam] Lind. **Hawaii's Japanese.** 1946. Two vols. in one

Condit, Ira M. **The Chinaman as We See Him and Fifty Years of Work for Him.** 1900

Conroy, Hilary. **The Japanese Frontier in Hawaii, 1868-1898.** 1953

Daniels, Roger, ed. **Anti-Chinese Violence in North America.** 1979

Daniels, Roger, ed. **Three Short Works on Japanese Americans.** 1979

Daniels, Roger, ed. **Two Monographs on Japanese Canadians.** 1979

Dooner, P[ierton] W. **Last Days of the Republic.** 1880

Flowers, Montaville. **The Japanese Conquest of American Opinion.** 1917

Gibson, O[tis]. **The Chinese in America.** 1877

Gulick, Sidney L[ewis]. **American Democracy and Asiatic Citizenship.** 1918

Hata, Donald Teruo, Jr. **"Undesirables,"** Early Immigrants and the Anti-Japanese Movement in San Francisco, 1892-1893. 1979

Irwin, Wallace. **Seed of the Sun.** 1921

Japan, Consulate General. **Documental History of Law Cases Affecting Japanese in the United States, 1916-1924.** Two vols. in one. 1925

Kachi, Teruko Okada. **The Treaty of 1911 and the Immigration and Alien Land Law Issue Between the United States and Japan, 1911-1913.** 1979

Kawakami, K[iyoshi] K[arl]. **The Real Japanese Question.** 1921

Kyne, Peter B. **The Pride of Palomar.** 1922

LaViolette, Forrest E[manuel]. **Americans of Japanese Ancestry:** A Study of Assimilation in the American Community. 1945

Lee, Rose Hum. **The Growth and Decline of Chinese Communities in the Rocky Mountain Region.** 1979

Li, Tien-Lu. **Congressional Policy of Chinese Immigration:** Or Legislation Relating to Chinese Immigration to the United States. 1916

Matsumoto, Toru. **Beyond Prejudice:** A Story of the Church and Japanese Americans. 1946

McClatchy, Valentine Stuart. **Four Anti-Japanese Pamphlets.** 1979

Mears, Eliot Grinnell. **Resident Orientals on the American Pacific Coast:** Their Legal and Economic Status. 1928

Millis, H. A. **The Japanese Problem in the United States.** 1915

O'Brien, Robert W. **The College Nisei.** 1949

Okubo, Mine. **Citizen 13660.** 1946

Shapiro, H[arry] L[ewis]. **Migration and Environment.** 1939

Steiner, Jesse Frederick. **The Japanese Invasion:** A Study in the Psychology of Inter-Racial Contacts. 1917

Sugimoto, Howard Hiroshi. **Japanese Immigration, the Vancouver Riots and Canadian Diplomacy.** 1979

Sung, Betty Lee. **Statistical Profile of the Chinese in the United States: 1970 Census.** 1975

Thompson, Richard Austin. The Yellow Peril, 1890-1924. 1979

U. S. House of Representatives, Committee on Immigration and Naturalization. **Japanese Immigration:** Hearings. 1921

U. S. House of Representatives, Select Committee Investigating National Defense Migration. **National Defense Migration:** Hearings. 1942

U. S. Department of State. **Report of the Honorable Roland S. Morris on Japanese Immigration and Alleged Discriminatory Legislation Against Japanese Residents in the U. S.** 1921

U. S. Department of War. **Final Report:** Japanese Evacuation from the West Coast, 1942. 1943

U. S. Senate, Joint Special Committee to Investigate Chinese Immigration. **Report.** 1877

Wing, Yung. **My Life in China and America.** 1909

Wong, Eugene. **On Visual Media Racism:** Asians in the American Motion Pictures. 1979

Wynne, Robert Edward. **Reaction to the Chinese in the Pacific Northwest and British Columbia, 1850-1910.** 1979

Yatsushiro, Toshio. **Politics and Cultural Values:** The World War II Japanese Relocation Centers and the United States Government. 1979

Young, Charles H., Helen R. Y. Reid and W. A. Carrothers. **The Japanese Canadians.** 1938

Zo, Kil Young. **Chinese Emigration into the United States, 1850-1880.** 1979